The Homemade Atheist

A FORMER
EVANGELICAL
WOMAN'S FREETHOUGHT
JOURNEY TO HAPPINESS

BETTY BROGAARD

Ulysses Press

Published in the U.S. by
ULYSSES PRESS
P.O. Box 3440
Berkeley, CA 94703
www.ulyssespress.com

ISBN13: 978-1-56975-784-0
Library of Congress Control Number 2009940346

Acquisitions Editor: Kelly Reed
Managing Editor: Claire Chun
Editor: Richard Harris
Editorial: Lauren Harrison, Kelly Winton
Cover design: DiAnna VanEycke
Cover photo: © istockphoto.com/dial-a-view
Production: Judith Metzener

Printed in Canada by Webcom

10 9 8 7 6 5 4 3 2 1

Distributed by Publishers Group West

To my sister and dear friend Dianne,
whose encouragement never faltered as I wrote this book.

Table of Contents

Foreword

My first exposure to the superb writings of Betty Brogaard came one memorable day on Amazon.com when the online megastore showcased, on its opening screen, Betty's first book, *Dare to Think for Yourself*. Because the theme of that book—atheism—was a subject near and dear to my heart, I clicked the link to see what all the excitement was about.

After reading a five-star review of Betty's newly published work, I saw, incredibly, that my own book on atheism was paired with Betty's in Amazon's "Better Together" program, giving customers a small discount if they purchased both of our books as a bundle. Since Amazon currently offers over four million titles for sale, my bundling with Betty—gosh, that sounds cozy!—was indeed an amazing coincidence.

But my good luck wasn't yet over. Only a few days thereafter, I received a personal e-mail from Betty herself, who likewise had seen the pairing of our books on Amazon. We agreed to trade copies of our work via U.S. mail. "I'll show you mine if you show me yours." There's no doubt that I got the better end of the exchange.

What makes Betty's writing so absorbing and informative—and just plain fun to read—is her extraordinary background. For a time, she was personal secretary to the famous television evangelist Garner Ted Armstrong. Armstrong, now deceased, was a dashing, quick-witted, slick-talking "man of God," whose Bible-based theology Betty, at the time, swallowed hook, line, and sinker. So, as you're reading the book you now hold, you should enjoy a feeling of confidence that the author truly knows her subject from the inside looking out, as well as from the outside looking in.

To me, Betty's personal experiences and insight make the crucial difference between this title and other, less impressive volumes on atheism. Just as soldiers in combat tend to place more credibility and trust in a commander-in-chief who has himself served in the military, a reader seeking to understand and overcome his religious indoctrination will be emboldened by Betty's "in the trenches," "battle-hardened" analysis of both sides in this theological "war." Betty's "weapons," however, are those of science, logic, diplomacy, and education.

Most books on atheism unfortunately transform an inherently fascinating debate into an unreadable and tedious grind. These "high-brow" books are a chore to read and were written essentially to further an academic's career within the university system rather than to communicate anything meaningful or important to readers. The result is that few books on atheism today are actually addressed to a popular audience. Her book beautifully fulfills a deep need for such a popular volume. I took immense pleasure and gratification in reading the pages of this marvelous book. I could simply relax and enjoy myself, without needing a twenty-digit calculator or an unabridged dictionary of foreign phrases to make sense of what I was reading. Thank you, Betty!

Although I personally have been an atheist for over thirty years and consider myself well-informed on the subject, Betty has opened my eyes to a wealth of new information in the pages that follow. Despite the common misperception that atheists know nothing of scripture, Betty's in-depth understanding of the Bible is dazzling to me. For example, I learned that God supposedly gave Moses *two* conflicting sets of Ten Commandments. Did you know that the second set of commandments warns us not to "boil a baby goat in its mother's milk"? That was certainly news to me—a commandment I'll strive to follow in my future goat boilings. If you are skeptical that such a silly rule is truly part of the biblical Ten Commandments, then you will be pleased that Betty provides detailed references and specific source citations throughout her well-researched text.

Much of what Betty says will be startling and difficult to accept by many religiously oriented readers. That's fine. Skepticism is good. Betty has thoroughly documented every quotation and every factual assertion in this book—a habit that other authors should emulate. Betty openly states that she doesn't want you to simply "take her word" for *anything*. She specifically rejects such a blind-faith philosophy or an "appeal to authority," even toward her own writings. Such a self-effacing attitude is refreshing and rare these days and, to me, further enhances the book's integrity.

My advice to you, the reader, would therefore be to check out Betty's statements. Put them to the test. Read the references she gives you. Look at every word Betty says under a cynical microscope. If you do this, then you will discover, as I did, that her facts are indeed facts and that her logical conclusions flow incontrovertibly from her firmly established premises. As President Reagan once said of Soviet leader Mikhail Gorbachev, we must "trust but verify." Betty welcomes your close scrutiny, because she has meticulously prepared a highly reliable volume that you can both trust *and* verify.

My own writings on atheism have enjoyed good success and robust sales. Fifty years from now, however, my greatest "claim to fame" may not be my own publications, but my being granted the privilege of introducing Betty's newest book to you—a book that is destined to become a freethought classic. There is much more I could say about this inspiring volume and its admirable author. But I hesitate for one critical reason: the author, as you will soon discover, speaks very well for herself.

David Mills
Author of *Atheist Universe*

Introduction

No god has ever spoken to me—not orally, not in a vision, a trance, or a dream. For many years, I thought one did through the book that Christians call "holy." I, however, now believe that the Holy Bible and all other autocratic books of scripture are human works. Contradictions, gross inaccuracies, absurdities, and failed prophecies in these volumes are among the reasons for my conclusion. They indicate that the Bible simply cannot be from any "perfect" spirit being. It is primarily fiction and myth. It is not messages from any supernatural entity to me personally or to anyone else.

I also now realize that predicaments, problems, and difficulties in my younger days were never solved by seeking guidance from God. In my opinion, the long hours of headache-producing fasts, agonizing prayer, and extensive Bible study were a waste of energy in trying to discover God's will. Circumstances, experience, and sometimes just plain common sense are the means that most often show me, now an unbeliever, answers to life's dilemmas. And without my knowing so, these were the same means that worked long before I laid aside my cloak of Christianity—even though I almost always gave the credit to

God when life's wrinkles smoothed out. I've learned that the greatest healers and problem solvers are time, contemplation, and, perhaps in certain situations, counseling with wise people who have no religious axes to grind.

After I finally acknowledged the Bible's inaccuracies, its discrepancies, etc., I moved on to investigate this whole god thing. Now, I admit, honestly and bluntly, that at present I don't believe in any supernatural being. There simply is no proof one way or another. If even one exists, why doesn't he/she/it speak to everyone in the same way and with the same message? After all, 1 Timothy 2:4 states quite clearly that "...God our Savior...wants all men to be saved and to come to a knowledge of the truth."

For far too long I never stopped to think, if this is true, why there would be hell and eternal punishing, separation from "him," or, as some believe, complete annihilation of unbelievers.

But doesn't "all" mean *all*? It seems to me that if God wants everyone to be saved but loses even one person, such a deistic plan has failed. That would make any deity less than perfect and, certainly, less than omniscient. If God can't even get everything he wants, then why should I think that I could?

Why did not a god or gods give us *clear* directives that every person on earth would have access to and understand in precisely the same way? Why are there so many different religions with their individual holy guidebooks? Why are there so many diverse views about what one so-called holy book means? Why are there so many different doctrines on the same subject from the same book?

Some claim that they have heard the voice of god. Some have even communicated to me that they themselves are god—and so am I! I've read books, including the Holy Bible, that say because some sort of god, usually referred to as masculine, has spoken to the authors, everyone should heed what he revealed to them. Ironically, I may agree in some small measure with what a god supposedly told some of those writers. My agreement, however, is not based on the authors' words or the so-called messages from any of their gods. It comes from the process of reason, research, common sense, and my own life experience.

Proof that there is even one god has never been objectively shown to me. And someone else's subjective experience—Moses', Elijah's, Jesus', the Apostle Paul's, John the Revelator's, Billy Graham's, the Pope's, yours, or anyone else's—is not proof enough for me. Why should I take the word of people who say that a god has spoken to them through whatever means? Where is the proof? I personally didn't hear him, her, it, or them. I certainly didn't get the same message they received by reading the same words they wrote or read. Why should I not simply accept their avowal of having received a message from a god as nothing more than a figment of their imagination? Perhaps for some people who fervently believe, there is simply a deep-seated need to believe and assuage their fear of death and punishment. Sometimes a desire to please, impress, or control others is the reason many people adopt belief.

The subject of atheism and its meaning has been covered eloquently and clearly by many freethinkers. My purpose, therefore, is not to reiterate what atheism is or what the word means. I suggest you read Dan Barker's *Losing Faith in Faith,* Earl Doherty's *The Jesus Puzzle,* Sam Harris' *The End of Faith,* David Mills' *Atheist Universe,* Bertrand Russell's *Why I Am Not a Christian,* and George H. Smith's *Atheism: The Case Against God,* among many, many other works.

At this juncture, I simply want you to know why humanism, agnosticism, and atheism appeal to more and more people who are dissatisfied with religion in general. My goal is to spotlight religion's negative impact usually through guilt, misinformation, and confusion in day-to-day lives of ordinary believers. My aim is to tell you how unbelief enhances the lives of many thinking people—more specifically, my own life.

In this book I have recounted circumstances and events that gradually produced my humanistic-nonbeliever perceptions. I also included much of my research as I explored religion in general, but especially Christianity.

My personal experiences have given me unique approaches to life just as yours have given you. Call it the school of hard knocks or simply the best teacher, experience through trial and error is how I and, indeed, civilization have progressed or regressed, succeeded or failed. And it is continual learning from practical experience coupled with self education that could change me into a better person, not fear of how a presumed god might punish me if I don't worship him.

Throughout this work, I most often quote from two translations of the Bible: the New International Version (NIV) which is considered a good, easy-to-read version, and the New American Standard Bible (NASB), rather academic in tone and considered by many as the most exact English translation available. I also quote several times from the familiar King James Version (KJV). I urge readers to compare various versions for their own enlightenment.

May you learn from the experience of reading this book.

—Betty Brogaard

Part 1

The Path to Unbelief

1

The Unbeliever's Happiness

Unbelief was not a "choice" for me. I did not decide between atheism and theism in the way I choose vanilla, strawberry, chocolate, or bubblegum flavors at the ice cream parlor. I progressed into agnosticism and finally humanistic atheism because of many religious questions that weren't being answered well enough for me. Through personal research, religion comparison, much contemplation, reason, and experience with believers and unbelievers alike, I evolved into unbelief.

I came to concur with the rational atheist who wrote, "I'm not a devotee of reason because I'm an atheist; rather, I'm an atheist because I'm a devotee of reason." The more I studied, the more the atheistic stance made sense to me. It sort of crept up on me.

So often we unbelievers, individually, feel very much alone because we are misunderstood and maligned by believers, including close friends, family members, and the general population. A recent *Newsweek* poll indicates, for example, that atheism is a definite impediment to a political career. Apparently, only a small percentage of Americans would vote for an otherwise qualified atheist for president.

Yet, many more would vote for any god believer, even if he or she were less qualified than an atheist running on the same ticket.

So it is very encouraging to me personally that many well-known people in various fields of endeavor have professed either an atheistic, humanist, or agnostic position. And, no, this is not a case of "misery loving company," for I am far from miserable with my unbelieving status. It is simply comforting to know that others, most of whom are much wiser, more educated, and more fearless than I, have come to the same conclusions that I have.

An Unexpected Conversion

What possible reason would a devoutly religious woman in her early sixties have for leaving Christianity? What could entice her to become an unbeliever and accept the usually despised label of atheist?

This conversion for me was a gradual process that began many years ago. Believe me, it wasn't planned.

Before we met, my late husband Fred and I had both been baptized into the Worldwide Church of God (WCG) in our respective home areas. This religion was considered a cult and, in my opinion realized with hindsight, rightly so. It was headed at that time by the "apostle" Herbert W. Armstrong and his handsome evangelist son Garner Ted. I applied and was accepted by the church's Ambassador College in Pasadena, California. I went there from Memphis, Tennessee, in the late 1950s. Fred entered the college from Wisconsin after a four-year stint in the Air Force and a semester or two in a Lutheran pre-seminary school. He had hoped to become a Lutheran pastor until he became acquainted with and intrigued by the Worldwide Church of God's literature and radio broadcasts.

Fred and I were married in 1964 at Ambassador College. Three years later, my husband was ordained as a minister in the cult and served in that capacity for about ten years. When rumblings of discontent began among some ministers and members of the WCG over certain doctrinal issues, we began an in-depth study of the cultic teachings that were being challenged. As a result, we saw that major beliefs we had held for such a long time indeed were wrong. In addition, we opened our eyes to the greed and immorality among some of the church hierarchy and left the organization amidst dire warnings of eternal punishment for abandoning the "true" church of god.

I continued my study and investigation of religion in general, but after about seven years of not attending any church, Fred and I joined a Lutheran Church in the Seattle, Washington, area. This was the denomination that Fred had been in before the WCG snagged him. The Lutheran Church, however, did not satisfy me, as my continued questions were not adequately answered. I nevertheless stayed in that denomination for fifteen years and tried to be a good Lutheran. I taught women's Bible studies and children's Sunday school, sang in the choir, and often performed for Sunday church services as a soloist. What kept me involved for so long? Primarily it was fearful chagrin that I could be wrong a second time about a religion and how my decision to leave would affect my husband and our marriage. Eventually, though, I could no longer pretend. I left Christianity and continued my study and research. My fear abated, and my marriage did not fall apart, although Fred remained a devout Christian in the Lutheran Church until he died in 2008.

After I left orthodoxy, I attended a Unitarian-Universalist fellowship for a few years. There I was introduced to diverse religious viewpoints, but I was unable to make any of them my own. I finally accepted the fact that I indeed had become an unbeliever, an atheist. Members of the church and many of my friends and relatives were shocked when I "came out of the atheist closet" with the publication of my first book. For me, atheism definitely was an unexpected conversion from Christianity.

Do Atheists Have a Belief System?

A few years ago, one of my in-laws was going through a financial and emotional rough spot. She was apparently questioning her own viewpoints about life and God. She asked me, "Betty, since you don't have a belief system, what is your goal in life?" She seemed to be wondering what possible happiness or purpose I can have without some sort of god in my life to direct me.

Her question surprised me as I realized that she simply had no understanding of me and my nonreligious perspective. You see, I do have a system of belief, or more accurately, a system of discovery. I describe it as a position of expanding certainty that no god exists. For me, reaching a decision, especially about religion, requires continually uncovering facts uncolored by feelings or emotion. That, in a nutshell, is my "system." My viewpoints are not static; they're dynamic. They grow, become clearer, and change with time and study. My position is definitely not a closed "belief system" as, for example, Christianity, Judaism, and Islam most often are.

As far as goals are concerned, each of us should determine what is important to us in life. Many succeed and many fail in the achievement of individual hopes and dreams. Life is frequently hard. It rarely flows smoothly for anyone. No one, from my point of view, is born to achieve purposes designed by an outside source—a god—before death. Our experiences, our environment, our health, our families, friends, and associates—everything and everyone that impact or touch our lives—contribute negatively, positively, or neutrally to what we do with the time we have.

Throughout our years here on earth, education increases not only through academic pursuits but also through everyday experience—if we allow ourselves to learn from it. Circumstances change. We may watch some of our plans and goals come to naught. At some point, we may need to switch goals altogether, expand or modify them, or take another path toward achieving them. Some people choose unrealistic or foolish objectives and make the same mistakes repeatedly.

So, basically, I informed my in-law concerning my present "belief system," as she put it, that I know (I don't simply "believe") that I exist. I interact as charitably as possible with others who also exist—not with an entity whom I cannot see, cannot dialogue with, cannot touch, and, apparently, even according to Christians, cannot understand because it is outside our physical realm. I tried to explain that my overall goal in life is not a set point in time or a particular achievement. It is reaching and passing milestones of understanding based on proven facts.

Real Goals or Calculating "Faith"?

I've noticed that there are certain people of various belief systems who may prefer the designation "spiritual" rather than "religious." (We'll speak more about this later.) Some of these individuals never have any earthly goals, especially in a long-term sense. They just "roll with the punches" through life, deceiving themselves into believing they are being directed by some sort of supernatural being or force. And they may even profess that they have no concern for how they will receive life's necessities. They have faith! But occasionally these people are reduced to begging.

They may ask outright for help at times or simply hint at their needs. And generous, compassionate people often will lighten their burdens with monetary gifts or other physical help. Then these individuals needing assistance may erroneously believe or, more than likely, indulge in the pretense that they were provided for because some "force"—usually a god or some "spiritual" entity—outside the physical plane moved others to come to their aid. They leave human compassion out of the picture altogether.

I wonder if some believers in dire straits accept what David, the alleged author of Psalm 37, wrote in Psalm 37:25:

> I was young and now I am old, yet *I have never seen the righteous forsaken or their children begging bread.* (NIV Study Bible—italic emphasis added)

That's quite a blanket declaration. People caught in the vortex of deprivation, especially through no fault of their own, after reading such Bible verses, may feel rather forsaken. They may believe they are horribly unrighteous. But perhaps David was simply not all that observant. On the other hand, didn't God inspire the writing of all the Bible? And isn't the Bible true in every respect? Think about it and decide for yourself if the children of the righteous never beg. These days throughout the world there are an awful lot of parents and children begging bread (or seeking a job or a home they can afford). Are they all "unrighteous"? Are all those who receive food for themselves and their families from food banks wicked people?

According to the Bible, they are, for Romans 3:10–12 (where the alleged Apostle Paul paraphrases verses from Psalm 14 and Psalm 53) states:

> There is no one righteous, not even one; there is no one who understands, no one who seeks God. All have turned away, they have together become worthless; there is no one who does good, not even one. (NIV)

Perhaps, then, David was correct in saying he had never seen the children of the righteous begging for bread since, according to Paul, no one is righteous—which would include you and me.

Before we move on to other things, I believe a more malignant and manipulative group of out-and-out moochers should be addressed at this point. They are the slick televangelists and fanatical Bible thumpers begging in "the name of Je-ee-sus."

They make their duped followers feel sinful and guilty if they don't sacrifice until it hurts. Yet some of these moochers themselves cheat the government as well as their followers, stage fake healings, and indulge in extracurricular activities that have nothing to do with the preaching or living of a so-called Christian Gospel. They drive expensive cars, wear designer clothing, and live in mansions. And, further, have you ever noticed that some TV evangelists especially seem to prefer white garments—to, perhaps, emphasize their "purity"? They preach before multitudes in impressive, grandiose settings. I'm fairly sure you could name several such infamous evangelizing performers as well as psychologists or marriage counselors. They believe, or at least lead others to believe, that they are directed by God for everyone else's benefit! They promise happy marriages, perfect children, and comfortable financial circumstances for all who heed what they preach and, of course, support their ministries with monetary gifts.

Those who follow this type of revered "guru" are gullible to say the least. They are convinced that they have been shown "the truth" through their esteemed leader. These unsuspecting dupes are persuaded that they will be protected, cared for, and safely ensconced in some future, paradisiacal promised land if they do their part with a good work ethic and support the guru's organization.

Many sincere seekers are enticed into an association of believers who make up the "true" Church of God. How do I know this? Because I was once a dupe of this type myself. I had the distorted view that God would provide my physical needs if I agreed with the guru's ideas about what so-called holy scripture meant. Oh, yes, and I had to work diligently in order to be faithful with tithes and large offerings. Then at the return of Jesus the Christ, whether I was dead or alive at the time, an eternity of unimagined, never-ending glory and joy would be mine! (You see, in this particular cult we believed that no one flew off immediately to heaven at death. We had to wait for the second coming of Christ and the resurrection.)

And what about pious, mooching priests, monks, and nuns who are supported by "the" church because they have taken a vow of poverty? Need I mention that among these clerical collared and cassocked people are those who can't control their perverted sexual desires for children even with the help of their Almighty God? And please understand that such predators are not limited to one specific denomination or even one gender. Some of these wretches, male and female, have shattered the lives of innocents not only through sexual exploitation but also through authoritative domination, cruelty, and greed.

Some have destroyed marriages within their own churches because they can't maintain their vow of celibacy or obey the commandments not to covet or commit adultery—again, even with the help of their God. And make no mistake about it, horrible offenses continually take place inside the hallowed walls of religious institutions.

Before leaving this subject, let's not forget the powerful politicians, multimillionaire business people, and sports icons who say they are Christians or at least religious. Yet, so many of these people in the public limelight get into prostitution, commit adultery, lie, cheat, or involve themselves in cruel, nefarious activities. Are they simply so important in their own eyes they think they can get way with such things—or are they simply stupid? I imagine the reasons are a combination of disgusting carnal factors including greed, lack of personal control over their own desires, and less love for their victims and families than for themselves.

Shouldn't we strive to learn from not only our own mistakes but those of others? Even though I still make blunders, I have learned and am still learning from past mistakes. Yes, from experience. One of my overriding goals is that learning will continue for the remainder of life. Part of my education may come because of other mistakes I will undoubtedly make simply because I am human. Since, however, I am not a masochist, I desire that most of my learning experiences will be through benign, personal efforts to understand more about myself, others, and indeed the universe—and, more importantly, without harming anyone else. There is so very much that I don't know or understand.

You're on Your Own

Unbelievers experience setbacks just as believers do, but we don't expect that a supernatural entity will make it all better for us if we put our trust in him, her, or it. When we "fall" because we have screwed up, have been wronged, or get knocked down through foolish decisions, rejection, debilitating illness, accident, or devastating loss of loved ones, we know that, if at all possible, getting up and moving forward again is up to us. And when help is given, we know who to thank: thoughtful, caring human beings, not a make-believe spiritual entity.

We don't all have the same physical and mental strengths. We don't all possess the same natural, inherited, or acquired abilities. We don't all have the same personalities. Depending, however, on the measure of mental acuity each of us possesses along with personal determination, interest, and encouragement from others at times, practically everyone is endowed with the capacity for achievement in varying degrees.

Consider the brilliant British physicist Stephen Hawking. He is on record as saying that he does not believe in a personal God. For example, on the *Larry King Live* TV program aired December 15, 1999, Professor Hawking was asked pointedly by the host: "Do you believe in God?"

Hawking replied, "Yes, if by God is meant the embodiment of the laws of the universe."

But his views about whether or not a god exists are not what makes this extraordinary man special. At age twenty-one, Professor Hawking was diagnosed with Amyotrophic Lateral Sclerosis (ALS), better known as Lou Gehrig's disease, a progressive, incurable motor neuron debility. Presently in his sixties, he has almost no physical power. Over the years as he has become more incapacitated by paralysis, he has learned to adjust. In his specially equipped, motorized wheelchair, he communicates through computerized instruments. He has authored numerous scientific papers and books. He has lectured to scientific communities throughout the world.

Professor Hawking is a remarkable human being, albeit physically flawed. Yet neither he nor anyone else was chosen by a spiritual entity for the accomplishment of particular tasks in life. I believe we develop through heredity, relationships, interests, willpower, and circumstances in our environments. We are all on this earth by some quirk of evolving nature and not because of the whims of an imaginary god. This puts everyone on more or less equal footing in that we can progress at our own speed according to our individual abilities, situations, and inclinations.

My Joy Comes from Doing, Not Believing

I've been told by religious people that sooner or later I will, at the final judgment, regret my godlessness. But no matter how many times I've heard this, I know that my years on earth for the most part have been good. I enjoy a simple, comfortable life but am not wealthy. I am most assuredly not a genius as Steven Hawking is. But, yes, from time to time I experience disappointments and adversity just as believers do.

Just like most people, I mourn the personal loss of loved ones because they leave a big void in my life, and I miss them. Recently my devout Christian husband lost his battle with a rare form of stomach cancer. Despite our religious differences, he was my hero; and I'm not ashamed to admit that I am struggling through this bereavement period because I am lonely, not because of my unbelief. I also cry with others, believers and unbelievers alike, who experience tragedy.

Increasingly, in spite of emotional setbacks, I still find joy in the freedom from arbitrary religious rules and "thou shalt nots." I take pleasure in helping others however I can, in doing my bit to protect the balance of nature, and in repairing the crumbling wall of separation between religion and the U.S. government. In whatever small ways I can help accomplish these things, I do them without thought of pleasing a god.

There is such deliverance in "doing good" because I want to and without the fear of hell and a vengeful spirit being punishing me if I don't. I don't worry about coming back after death in a different body, as the Buddhists and Hindus teach, because I didn't "get it right" in a previous life. I cherish my emancipation from every religious or philosophical organization that tells me what is "good" or good for me. Exercising my power of self-determination without trampling over others and without a sense of guilt contributes much to my joy and happiness.

Before and After

I studied the Bible avidly when I was a Christian. And that was the big reason I was not very happy in the believers' world. You see, despite the wonderful proclamations and assurances in it, I also knew what "holy" scripture said God would do to me or those I love if we didn't meet his confusing criteria. I knew what he had already done, according to the Bible, to those who displeased him. I was much too serious, too inquisitive, and too informed about the so-called Word of God for my own peace of mind as a Christian.

Having been reared by a religious mother and indoctrinated primarily by two legalistic religious organizations—one cultic and one, later in life, orthodox—I can attest to the fact that for years my religious training had a profoundly detrimental effect on me psychologically. I was never "good" enough. I couldn't "tame my tongue," which seemed constantly getting me into trouble. I could never do enough to thank Jesus for giving his life for me (even though I was taught that "works" do not count for righteousness and that we cannot pay for salvation). In fact at one point in my life I counseled with my husband, then an ordained minister, about being baptized a second time because I was afraid the first baptism didn't take. I feared that I might not have the Holy Spirit. I didn't have success in becoming perfect, as Jesus admonishes in Matthew 5:48. That's how insecure I became as I strove for completeness in my Christian walk. Talk about lack of confidence!

As a young Christian adult, I received many mixed messages from studying "the Word." This diverse information from reading the Bible and books about the Bible, listening to various ministers and their differing opinions caused much emotional turmoil for me. My efforts to understand the "truth" about how God wanted me to live stirred up many questions about the Bible's contradictions and its validity for my life. Finally, after much study and religion comparison as well as counseling with various ministers as I tried to make sense of it all, I questioned even the existence of a God who seemed incapable of making his instructions crystal clear.

In spite of all my personal doubts for many years, however, I did feel privileged to be a Christian, to be "chosen" by almighty God. For most of my life I believed what Jesus supposedly said in John 6:44: "No one can come to me unless the Father who sent me draws him...." (NIV Study Bible).

But the more I studied, the more questions I had and the more I wondered: What if he didn't truly "draw" me to him? What if I was just an interloper? After all, as I had been taught, because he is so far above us and his thoughts are not the same as ours, we can't understand the mind of God. We can't thoroughly appreciate his methods for bringing about his magnificent plan.

No wonder I was so unsettled in the Christian world.

Nevertheless, as a believer I found certain pleasure in the company of other sincere Christians. I enjoyed participating in the "communion of the saints," which was stressed as paramount to staying on the "straight and narrow path."

When I look back to that time in my life, I see little difference in the attitudes of members of the cult I was in for twenty years and those of the orthodox church where I was a member for fifteen years. In both organizations, we fed off one another's self-righteous piety and assurance that we knew and followed "the truth." We had, if not the "only" truth, the "best" truth.

I remember the words of one sweet, well-meaning, little old Christian lady who approached my husband and me after we had left the cultic church and joined the Lutheran Church. She took our hands in hers and said, "I'm so glad you finally saw that we're right!"

Having put all that behind me, I now enjoy participating in the "communion of nonbelievers," that is, the sharing of a meal or ideas, books, and experiences. I treasure the fellowship with those who are not offended by different points of view and who do not threaten, warn, shame, or preach to me about displeasing a more than likely make-believe deity. I am grateful that I no longer fear a being who could send me off to a place of eternal torture or separation from him because I used my brain and concluded through research and study that he is probably nonexistent. Simply stated, I no longer worry about fulfilling requirements for salvation. I merely do the best I can to enhance life for myself as well as for all those with whom I come in contact.

I confess, therefore, that when I was a Christian, I was much less happy than I am now as an unbeliever. Paramount in my thinking as a cultic believer and later as an orthodox Christian was my fear of not being accepted into the kingdom of God or into heaven. I was immensely earnest in striving for the high ideal, the lofty New Testament standard of perfection that the Biblical "savior" supposedly sets for his followers in the "Sermon on the Mount" (Matt. 5:48).

And, yes, I still want to be the best, most loving, most sincere person I can possibly be in life. I no longer beat myself up mentally or emotionally, however, when I fail to practice my own personal live-and-let-live standards. And I do fail in that regard far more often than I like to admit. As said before, I am human; but now I'm relaxed over that fact.

Materialism

One morning at breakfast a few years ago, my husband and I engaged in discussion with a guest in our home about philosophical and religious differences. My husband said during the course of our conversation, "For example, Betty is a thoroughgoing materialist."

I had never applied that label to myself, but I recognized that he was correct. I also understood that he did not believe that I have an excessive desire for material possessions.

What my husband meant is that I see life as wholly the product of natural processes. I believe that everything that exists and all that happens in the universe outside humanity's control or interference can be explained, given enough time and scientific evidence, in terms of the laws of the universe and nature. I believe nothing can be dogmatically determined or proven in terms of the action or the intervention of a supernatural entity.

In my opinion, nothing exists but matter. This includes even energy, which, in the simplest of terms, is the capacity for activity. I base this on my limited understanding of what some branches of science have concluded:

That the entire material universe is made from energy;

That energy cannot be created;

That energy cannot be destroyed.

Now some religious scientists have speculated that "energy," then, is god! They may define "god" as a spirit entity, a force, or a source without beginning or end and with absolute power. But I require proof that this is so, just as I require proof that the personal God of the Bible exists.

Mark Perakh is professor emeritus of physics at California State University, Fullerton. In his book *Unintelligent Design*, Perakh states:

> Whatever this or that scientific theory concludes, it never points either to or against the hypothesis of a creator at work.
>
> For example, the theory of the inflationary big bang...may be correct or wrong, but in either case the existence of a creator may be either hypothesized or denied, the grounds for both propositions being beyond scientific consideration...
>
> If a scientific theory were to assert that the universe is eternal, it would not in any way contradict the hypothesis that there is God who is transcendental, who has established the laws of physics, and who rules the universe. Equally, it would not contradict the hypothesis that there is no transcendent entity beyond the universe, or that there is a transcendent supernatural entity which does not care at all about the universe. Science is not equipped to solve that problem and is not supposed to.
>
> If science asserts that the universe had a beginning, it does not either prove or disprove the existence of a creator, or any views as to what kind of a creator it could be....

Admitting my lack of scientific knowledge and education, I tend not to concur entirely with Professor Perakh's statements that the existence of a creator are "beyond scientific considerations," that science is not equipped to solve this problem, and that it "is not supposed to." Whether it is "supposed to" or not, it often does.

For example, Charles Darwin did not set out to prove the existence or nonexistence of god. His scientific observations and study, however, did introduce the theory of evolution, which does not enhance a belief in a creating god. And please keep in mind that "theory" is, in science, more than a speculative view. It is an explanatory system of ideas based on general principles independent of assumptions. It is an account of a particular subject based on reason and experiment. We accept the theory of music and the theory of mathematics; why not the theory of evolution?

Darwin wrote at length about how his ideas changed in a subsection of his autobiography titled "Religious Belief." He was trained as an Anglican minister but never ordained because he was offered a place on the *Beagle* expedition first. On the voyage, he says, he was "quite orthodox," but doubts arose while writing *The Origin of Species,* and he gradually turned to "skepticism and rationalism" during the last part of his life and became "content to be an agnostic." His discoveries changed his beliefs, not vice versa.

Nevertheless, I do expressly agree with Professor Perakh that "religious beliefs by and large are not based on rational arguments... [T]hey have little to do with ...scientific proofs."

Just as surely, I agree with Richard Dawkins in *The God Delusion*: "The presence or absence of a creative super-intelligence is unequivocally a scientific question, even if it is not in practice—or not yet—a decided one. So also is the truth or falsehood of every one of the miracle stories that religions rely upon to impress multitudes of the faithful" (page 59).

Until there is indisputable, scientific evidence that a god truly exists, I remain a materialist.

Happiness: A Reward for Belief?

Believers, somewhat like my aforementioned in-law, may ask, "What is your hope, your goal? How can you be happy when you don't believe in an afterlife?"

In his book, *Atheism: The Case Against God,* George H. Smith (one of my freethinking heroes) astutely notes that "...there is a gross dishonesty involved in offering happiness as a motivation for believing in a god. Theists who appeal to happiness as a reward for belief display a shocking disregard for intellectuality and the pursuit of truth."

A dear friend recently gave me a book by Andre Comte-Sponville titled *The Little Book of Atheist Spirituality.* Even though I don't agree with—or frankly, even understand— everything the author advocates, I found his comments concerning hope quite intriguing. He says on page 53:

> We usually think of serenity as the absence of fear, but it is also the absence of hope; thus, it frees the present moment for action, knowledge and joy!...To wish only for what depends on us (to *want*), is to give ourselves the means of making it happen. To wish for what does not depend on us (to *hope*) is to condemn ourselves to powerlessness and resentment...The wise act; the foolish hope and tremble. The wise live in the present, wishing only for what is (acceptance, love) or what they can bring about (will)...It is not hope that sets us free; it is truth. It is not hope that helps us live; it is love.

I had to read the above section several times before it finally sank in and I remembered the mindset I had when I was a believer. As a Christian, I felt totally unprepared for the day if I didn't pray on my knees for guidance. I felt something dreadful might happen if I didn't ask the God I so fervently believed in (or wanted to believe in) for protection of my loved ones and me. I asked him to keep me from sinning, to place a guard on my mouth, and to keep me from inadvertent offenses I might commit unknowingly. I would send up little thought prayers for myself and others throughout the day and hope that God would hear and answer my prayers. I didn't know it at the time, but prayer was for me like a superstitious rabbit's foot; and I didn't leave home without it!

If, perchance, this day is my last, it holds no dread for me. I know that my life has been full and in many ways privileged simply because I was born in a comparatively free country. I have not fought in wars or battled physically for my life or that of a loved one—unless you count the eighteen months at my darling husband's side trying to find a way to cure him of that dreadful cancer that finally ripped away his life.

I have not yet lived in a disaster-stricken area or a war-torn nation, as so many in the world do today. I agonize vicariously with them; but I can only imagine what it's like to lose everything—family, home, livelihood, parts of my body, the will to live—everything!

I have experienced, however, much of what humanity does during a lifetime. I have suffered rejection and encountered favor. Ridicule has torn me apart, but self-acceptance has made me stronger. I know from experience what being poor is and how much better it is to have a modicum of prosperity. I understand disappointment as well as satisfaction, failure as well as success. I have lived through fear and acquired courage.

I have agonized over the deaths of loved ones and have gradually healed with memories of the good times we had together. I have been tortured by loneliness and comforted with companionship. I have endured physical pain and have found sufficient relief to keep going. I have been assailed with depression and confusion and gained contentment and insight.

But unlike most of humanity, I and the freethinkers with whom I'm acquainted know the elation of living free of religious chains that bind so many believers to unproven tenets of faith and false hopes as well as fear of punishment in this life or the next. Having no affiliation with any church or religious organization, I now greet most days with anticipation.

I do not deny that some people feel happy and fulfilled because of their Christian beliefs. But I must also point out that some devout non-Christians feel happy and fulfilled because of their Hindu, Muslim, Buddhist, Taoist, and other religious persuasions or philosophies just as Christians do. With all the myriad differences in and means of worship, it is only logical to conclude that they can't all be true; but they all may be wrong.

The continual and purposeful "pursuit of truth" has become one of the delights of my life and is a treasured source of fulfillment for me as an unbeliever. My wish, indeed my enduring goal, is to understand more today than I did yesterday. And this expectation bestows on me immeasurable happiness.

2

Can Adherence to the Bible Bring Real Happiness?

Having been a sincere, practicing believer for most of my adult life, I speak from experience when I say that the Christian majority proclaims happiness for themselves because they believe they're saved from sin and from eternal damnation. They say they're happy because they have a personal relationship with Jesus (whatever that entails).

Yet ongoing observation and study show me that the happiest believers are those who don't comprehend that their Bible was put together over many centuries and that not one word of it was actually penned by Jesus Christ. Devout, fundamentalist Christians claim happiness because they profess belief in what the Bible says or, more than likely, in what the church teaches about the Bible.

Most believers don't seem to know what the book on which Christianity is based actually teaches or that it is riddled with discrepancies and absurdities. Why aren't they bothered by the fact that there are different accounts of the life of Jesus in the Gospels of the New Testament? Most Christians believe the gospels were written by men directly guided by a perfect God who presumably eschews confusion. Had I been less observant, less studious, less inquisitive, and even less sincere about discovering religious "truth," I would probably still be a Christian.

A majority of believers don't seem to know why their church requires obedience to its particular tenets of faith or its "tradition" when other churches teach something different. For example, during Lent a couple of years ago I asked a Catholic acquaintance why her church requires abstaining from meat and eating fish on Friday. She looked puzzled and said, "I don't know." I think that's rather interesting as, personally, I want to know why something is required of me before I agree to do it. We didn't pursue the subject further. I, however, can't help but think that she participates in certain religious rites and traditions simply to be on the safe side and because that's what she was taught to do.

So What about "Tradition"?

Some denominations place more emphasis on their "tradition" than they do on any so-called Word of God. You'll have to ask them why they do this. Perhaps it's because the church hierarchy is their "supreme court," and whatever they say goes—no matter what holy scripture seems to teach or how others might interpret that book.

The Catholic Church, for example, says that there is no problem with the church officially defining a doctrine that does not explicitly appear in scripture—as long as the teaching is not in contradiction to scripture. Catholics, and Episcopalians, too, by and large, probably don't know that Matthew 23:9 says, "...do not call anyone on earth 'father,' for you have one Father, and he is in heaven" (NIV). Tradition or not, calling a priest "Father" violates a biblical prohibition.

If Catholics and Episcopalians knew this, would they call their priests "Father"? Or perhaps, if they're aware of that verse, they simply feel that this is "unreasonable literalism." This is a fine illustration of how religious leaders pick and choose from "holy" scripture what they teach people to obey or not obey and what they themselves profess to obey or not obey.

If this is truly a New Testament command from Jesus that we are to call *no one* Father on this earth, what should we call the men who sired us? Maybe "Daddy" is okay, or perhaps "Pa" or "Papa." (Or is the latter reserved for the Catholic pope?) Maybe just plain "sir" or the man's given name would do. If you believe the Bible is the inerrant word of God, you might need to find an acceptable appellation other than "Father" for your human male parent.

Is Public Prayer Productive?

Happy Christians may also need to consider the widespread custom of starting meetings and gatherings of whatever nature with prayer, even if religion is not the subject of the event. Notice that according to the Bible (Matt. 6:6—NIV), Jesus tells his disciples: "...*when you pray*, go into your room, close the door and pray to your Father, *who is unseen*."

That same verse in the New American Standard Bible says: "But you, *when you pray*, go into your inner room, close your door and *pray to your Father who is in secret*, and *your Father who sees what is done in secret will reward you*" (italic added for emphasis).

In today's climate of religious fanaticism in America, it's more politically correct than ever to say you are a Christian believer. U.S. and state senators and representatives, school board members, and city, county, and other public officials insist on at least a generic prayer at the beginning of their gatherings. I wonder if they really believe that addressing an unseen, unspecified entity is efficacious in the successful performance of their duties and achievement of their opposing goals.

Some people are highly offended if prayers are not offered at religious or political meetings, special occasions, or before meals. For several years I was employed in a medical clinic. At my first "employee appreciation dinner" there, I wondered why a Catholic nun was asked to give the invocation before we ate. I didn't even know why she was in attendance, but that action surprised and somewhat annoyed me. Sitting quietly with unbowed head while the prayer was given, I thought to myself, "What have I gotten myself into?"

I learned gradually that most employees and doctors at the clinic were either Catholic or Lutheran. But other belief systems, such as Missionary Alliance, Unitarianism/Universalism, and even Islam, were also represented. Some attended nondenominational fellowships or mega-churches with a charismatic bent. As far as I know, I was the lone unbeliever. I resolved not to let that be known, for experience had taught me that atheists, for the most part, are considered evil by the religious. I had slipped on occasion by making "unorthodox" remarks; and believe me, they were not pleasant experiences.

For the next couple of years I didn't attend those dinners. It was not because of prayers that might be said but simply because I usually don't enjoy such affairs. Later, when I did attend, I noticed that no prayer was offered before the meal was served. I don't know whether some non-Catholic complained or not. But I did wonder if those who needed to pray before they ate did so silently. If not, why not? Don't they believe their God supposedly "hears" even unspoken prayers?

That's one of the reasons I can't understand all the folderol about why oral, public prayer is so necessary to some religious people. Perhaps bowing one's head and closing one's eyes while another prays on their behalf is the greatest "witness" they have to their belief that a god exists. And, of course, when an individual is asked to "lead us in prayer," it's like being Moses on the mountain.

If group attendees really are sincere believers, however, perhaps each one should make more personal time for private prayer *before* the meeting or assembly. Somehow, a generic public prayer seems inadequate for covering all the bases of the various religious and/or political persuasions.

How many professing Christians know what verse 7 in Matthew 6 says? "…[W]hen you pray, do not keep on babbling like pagans for they think they will be heard because of their many words" (NIV).

Catholic priests often ignore this supposedly direct commandment of Jesus against repetitious babbling. After confession by the sinner and subsequent forgiveness, the priest may assign penance to the confessor in the form of prayers—so many "Hail Marys" or "Our Fathers," laps around the rosary. Of course, I do understand that such penance is not done for "forgiveness." Rather, penance is an act of self-punishment and atonement for whatever sins one has committed. But this type of prayer still entails foolish repetition, which is one definition of babbling.

I suppose, if such activity makes people feel better about themselves, who am I to gainsay? Personally, when I do or say something that offends another, I may apologize to that individual, make amends if possible, or simply try not to give offense in the future. But I don't agonize over my humanness. My current method regarding forgiveness and atonement is just as productive to me as prayer ever was; and now I don't carry around a load of guilt.

Every Sunday at church services, many believers intone the Lord's Prayer which, strictly speaking, is only a teaching model *for* prayer. Most probably give little thought to the words they recite. This and other prayers prepared for them in their denomination's devotional material plus the rote "grace" prayer before meals (and also after meals in some religious circles) may be the only ones they ever use except in crisis situations.

Humility, a Lost Christian Attribute?

I wonder how many Christians know the attitude they should have if they're to enter God's Kingdom or heaven. Do they understand that, according to "holy" scripture, they, perhaps, should consider themselves as worms, even maggots, as did Bildad the Shuhite in the book of Job:

> How...can a man be righteous before God? How can one born of a woman be pure? If even the moon is not bright and the stars are not pure in his eyes, how much less man, who is but a maggot—a son of man, who is only a worm! (Job 25:2–6—NIV)

Some believers may point out that Bildad, along with Eliphaz the Temanite and Zophar the Naamathite, was rebuked by Job's Lord for mouthing, as the footnotes in one Bible version say, "many correct and often beautiful creedal statements, but without living knowledge of the God they claimed to honor."

But do most Christians today have "living knowledge" of the God they claim to worship? Is this even possible regarding an entity who can't be understood or whose existence can't even be proven? Believers say they simply rely on "faith"—belief without logical proof. Faith, to me, seems little different from hope. In fact, some dictionaries and thesauruses list *hope* as a synonym for *faith*.

The above cited verses from Job 25, of course, are a metaphorical comparison between the presumed greatness of the God of the Bible and the overall ineptitude of mere mortals. We all know that no human being is actually a worm or a maggot. But lest someone think that because the above verses are "Old Testament" and, therefore, not applicable to "New Testament" believers, this essential Christian attitude of abject humility and worthlessness is reiterated with less offensive language in Luke 14:11 as a warning: "For everyone who exalts himself will be humbled, and he who humbles himself will be exalted."

And then there are these verses in James 4 (NASB): "God is opposed to the proud, but gives grace to the humble" (James 4:6b); "Humble yourselves in the presence of the Lord, and He will exalt you" (James 4:10).

Some of our political leaders openly flaunt the badge of Christianity in a not-so-humble attitude. Televangelists and leaders of various denominations make idiotic pronouncements with hostility and vitriol. Should not they heed these "humble" verses if they truly believe the Bible? I, quite frankly, see very little humility between all the different Christian denominations as they bicker continuously over who's right and who's wrong about doctrine. Note the Biblical admonition recorded in Ephesians 4:2–4:

> Be completely *humble and gentle;* be patient, bearing with one another in love. Make every effort to keep the *unity of the Spirit* through the bond of peace…one Lord, one *faith,* one *baptism*…. (NIV—italic emphasis added)

But, really, how can there be "unity of the Spirit" when there are so many different beliefs garnered from the same book? Why are there so many "faiths" or doctrines, so many opinions about baptism, communion, and so on? Can all these differences be approved by a God of the universe? Does he not have a standard to which he holds all believers? (Chapter 6 of this book outlines some of the varying Christian viewpoints.)

In a recent discussion with one sincere Christian gentleman about these very questions, he told me there are, despite the different doctrines, certain "core beliefs" that every Christian must hold. Other beliefs are only peripheral. When I asked him if he would write down for me what these core beliefs are, he replied, "Well, I'll think about that and get back to you." I'm still waiting for his list.

After this discussion, I did a bit of independent research on "core Christian beliefs." And guess what: Christian churches don't even agree on what beliefs are *absolutely necessary* for salvation! Some denominations list as few as three or five; others record as many as twelve or more. One Catholic list enumerated twenty-one beliefs a person must hold in order to be saved. Even a declaration of monotheism cannot stand alone as a "core belief" according to the New Testament book of James: "You believe there is one God. Good! Even the demons believe that—and shudder" (Jas. 2:19—NIV).

My study left my head swimming, and I was more convinced than ever that religion does not have concrete answers regarding how a person should live or what a person *must* believe for salvation.

Are Christians Slaves?

Quite a number of years ago, when I was still a sincere Christian and working as secretary in the church office, I had a rare dialogue about "holy scripture" with my Lutheran pastor. Toward the end of that conversation, I mentioned to him that I felt honored to be a "slave" of God. I was quite taken aback when he exhibited offense at this. "*No*," he emphasized, "we are not slaves; we are free from sin!"

Truthfully, I was surprised by his outburst and wondered if he, perhaps, didn't remember what the following verse says:

> ...now that you have been set free from sin and *have become slaves to God*, the benefit you reap leads to holiness, and the result is eternal life. (Rom. 6:22 NIV—italic emphasis added)

I actually thought at the time of that encounter with my pastor that I *had been* a slave to sin before baptism. Then, Jesus "bought" me, and I became God's slave. This minister of the Word, however, didn't even attempt an explanation of that Bible verse. He suddenly remembered he had an appointment to keep. In light of his opposition, I don't think he knew how to explain what I had mentioned. In fact, after that he avoided any personal discussion of the Bible with me.

With my current understanding and a touch of irony, I now agree with him that human beings are not slaves to any god—unless they make themselves such—and should not be slaves to other human beings. But, of course, that Christian preacher and I still have different reasons for our similar opinions.

Since that little episode in my life as a Christian, I've discovered that very few conservative preachers want to discuss belief or doctrine or answer questions concerning scripture. Oh, yes, most are comfortable with visiting shut-ins, giving communion, performing weddings and funerals, preaching their canned sermons on Sunday morning, and indoctrinating young people and potential adult church members in catechism classes. But, please, don't ask them any serious questions about controversial Bible verses. Don't ask them to explain doctrines of their church and why they differ from the doctrines of other churches!

The Immortal Soul and Everlasting Hellfire

We hear much about an "immortal soul" in Christian circles. Ancient religious leaders, long before Christianity came into vogue, concocted the concept of an eternal soul separate from the body. This idea emerged because of evolving humanity's innate fear of death and the desire to live forever.

But if the soul can be destroyed, it can't be immortal. According to the Bible, you see, the soul apparently is not eternal but can be "destroyed." Notice:

> Do not be afraid of those who kill the body but cannot kill the soul. Rather, be afraid of the One who can destroy *both the soul and the body in hell*. (Matt. 10:28—NASB—italic emphasis added)

So, if the body and the soul can be destroyed in hell, then how can such cruelty as eternal, that is, never ending, punishment be carried out by a loving, compassionate God? (Besides, I didn't even know that the actual "body" ever went to hell *or* to heaven. If it does, then what is that in the coffin when it becomes necessary for an exhumation of a corpse sometimes years after actual death?)

One of the first verses in the Bible that I memorized as a Christian was Romans 6:23 which says, "For the wages of sin is death, but the gift of God is eternal life in Christ Jesus our Lord" (NIV Study Bible).

I don't remember when I began to wonder about the truth of this verse since the standard Christian definition for the wages of sin is not really death but is, in essence, eternal *soul-life* in hell or in some outpost of separation from God. Many preachers today, you see, no longer designate "hellfire" as eternal punishment. They, instead, say that separation from God forever is the sentence for an unrepentant sinner's soul. This probably sounds better to them than being burned eternally with unquenchable fire. It doesn't portray their God as quite so inhumane.

A letter from a Floridian reader was printed in the "Letter Box/ Freethought Mailbag" section of Volume 22, No. 5 of *Freethought Today,* published by the Freedom From Religion Foundation, Inc. This freethinker stated in part:

> Immense amounts of time and energy are expended in religious organizations dealing with [the survival of] nonexistent souls [after the death of the body]. Would…time and energy not be better expended solving real problems, like how to make sure that all humans get enough to eat and how to provide all humans with warm and pleasant surroundings in which to live?

I would like to raise my voice and say, "Yes and Amen" to that. There has never been any scientific evidence that human beings or other animal species possess an immortal soul. Notable ancient and contemporary freethinkers as well as some Christians of yesteryear and today have rejected or at least seriously questioned the doctrine of the immortality of the soul. Perhaps in a few hundred more years (if humanity hasn't destroyed the earth by then) science will prove without a doubt that humans don't have souls. But even then, the church may cling to its outmoded beliefs simply because it wants the souls of "sinners" punished without benefit of parole, forever and ever and ever and ever and—well, you get the point.

What Is Heaven Really Like?

Do Bible believers waiting to be reunited with deceased spouses realize what Jesus purportedly said about that subject?

The Sadducees, who did not believe in a resurrection or an immortal soul, allegedly asked him a "trick" question regarding a hypothetical situation. They wanted to know whose wife a woman would be at the resurrection if she had married legitimately seven times during her earthly life.

> Jesus replied, "You are in error because you do not know the Scriptures [apparently the Jews in Jesus' day didn't know them any better than average believers do today] or the power of God. At the resurrection people will neither marry nor be given in marriage; they will be like the angels in heaven." (Matt. 22:29—NASB)

There are Old Testament scriptures, including Isaiah 26:19, Daniel 12:2, and Job 19:25–27, that falsely, in my opinion, indicate a resurrection which the Sadducees did not believe would take place. They must have been the liberal, freethinking skeptics of their day.

I haven't found an Old Testament scripture to which Jesus refers that would corroborate his avowal that there will be no marriage at the resurrection. Remember that the only scripture the Jews had during Jesus' alleged lifetime was the Old Testament. I assume, therefore, that Jesus means the angels are asexual. I can't, however, find a biblical reference to what angels are like in that sense either. In fact, there are believers who hold the opinion that angels *are* sexual creatures because of Genesis 6:1–2:

> When men began to increase in number on the earth and daughters were born to them, the sons of God saw that the daughters of men were beautiful, and they married any of them they chose. (NIV Study Bible)

Some Christians think the "sons of God" in the above verses refer to angels and that the "daughters of men" are humans. Most students of the Bible these days, however, do not hold that opinion and believe this verse refers to sexual intercourse between human males and females. A number of commentaries and Bible footnotes even admit that intermarriage and cohabitation between angels and human beings are commonly mentioned in ancient mythologies. Could it be that the Bible itself is myth? Some scholars do state that expressions in "holy" scripture regarding "sons of God" do not *always* mean "angels" but *can* refer to human beings or "godly" men and that "daughters of men" *can* refer to "sinful" women. (Well, of course, the women are always to blame, aren't they?)

Even in *The Expositor's Bible Commentary* regarding Matthew 13 through 28, D. A. Carson states that at the resurrection everyone will be "…capable of loving all and [will be] the object of the love of all—as a good mother today loves all her children and is loved by them" (page 462).

In other words, a wife or husband will not love their former earthly spouses any more than they love anyone else in the Kingdom of God. It seems that all relationships will be platonic.

Another fact that some misinformed Christians may find hard to accept is that when "good" people, that is, other Christians, die they do not become angels in heaven. Not even babies and children do. I have read many touching poems and stories and seen motion pictures, TV programs, and even media advertisements (showing half-clad, voluptuous young women with wings) portraying this falsehood.

The 1946 movie classic *It's a Wonderful Life* comes to mind. This film is about an angel, once a married man on earth, who shows a discouraged, suicidal businessman what life would have been like for his friends and family had he (the businessman) never been born. In doing so, the angel, whose name is Clarence, finally earns his wings! The sentiment is admittedly appealing, but the truth is that the Bible does not teach it.

We are familiar with artwork of cherubs portrayed as chubby, winged Gerber babies of, perhaps, one or two years old or younger. If one believes the Bible, however, cherubs are formidable created beings with more than one face and at least four wings. The seraphim, another type of angel in the Bible, may have six wings. Some angels have faces like animals. If I encountered such creatures, I'd be scared out of my wits.

To find out what the Bible actually says about these alleged spirit beings, look up the words angel, cherubim, seraphim, archangel, and living creatures in a concordance, Bible dictionary, or Bible commentary. You'll be surprised.

The Matter of Forgiveness

How many Christians realize that *forgiveness* of those who have offended or sinned against them is a prerequisite for being forgiven themselves? This is a tough requirement for anyone, since people in this world do rotten things that affect us personally, nationally, or ethnically time after time. But I wonder how many Christians truly live by or even strive to abide by the following New Testament injunction:

> …[I]f you forgive men when they sin against you, your heavenly
> Father will also forgive you. *But if you do not forgive men their sins, your
> Father will not forgive your sins.* (Matt. 6:14,15—NIV Study Bible—italic
> emphasis added)

Does that mean even if an interceding priest grants you forgiveness, God still won't forgive you unless you personally have forgiven the one who has sinned against you? Or is the priest's pronouncement of forgiveness good enough? ("Priestly" denominations probably have that worked out even though Romans 8:34 declares that only Jesus Himself is the intercessor—not a priest or a minister, not dead people made "saints" by the church, and not even "Holy Mother Mary.")

Even as a member of the Lutheran Church I always had misgivings about the efficacy of a mere man forgiving my sins against God. Toward the beginning of the Sunday liturgy, after the congregation confessed in unison its sins of the previous week (or of any intervening time since one attended church services, I suppose), the minister then would stand and say:

> Almighty God in his mercy has given His Son to die for you and for His sake forgives you all your sins. As a called and ordained servant of the Word, *I therefore forgive you all your sins* in the name of the father and of the Son and of the Holy Spirit. (Italic emphasis added)

In the Lutheran Church not only does one receive forgiveness by God himself, but also from a "called and ordained servant of the Word." In some Lutheran services this is watered down a bit by having the preacher merely "announce" the grace of God.

Women, Salvation, and Faith

I don't think the admonition to wives in Ephesians 5:24 goes over too well these days with most women. According to this verse, a wife must submit to her husband *in everything*. There is no provisional exception even if the husband is a womanizer or bisexual who could expose his spouse to deadly sexually transmitted diseases. Even if he is an abuser or a total dunderhead, the husband is the "head" of the family—and that's that.

And I imagine that more Christian men take seriously the instructions to females in 1 Timothy 2:11–14 than do most postmodern women—especially some of those female preachers I've seen on TV:

> A woman must quietly receive instruction with *entire submissiveness*. But I [Paul] do not allow a woman to *teach or exercise authority* over a man, but to remain quiet...[I]t was not Adam who was deceived, but the woman being deceived, fell into transgression. (NASB—italic emphasis added)

And these verses bring up another question in my mind. Didn't both Eve *and* Adam eat the "apple"? (By the way, the Bible does not say that the forbidden fruit was an apple.) Couldn't Adam have just said, "no"?

But moving on, if you can believe Genesis 2:16–17, Adam had been told personally by his creator not to eat of the tree of the knowledge of good and evil even *before* Eve existed! We are taught that Eve was deceived by Satan in the form of a serpent, the "master of deception." Adam, therefore, if he wasn't deceived through Eve, his merely human partner, just blatantly disobeyed God his Maker. And isn't that worse than being "deceived"?

Verse 15 of that same section of "holy" scripture might be just as offensive to some Christian women of current times and give pause for reflection as well:

> ...[W]omen will be preserved [or saved] through the bearing of children if they continue in faith and love and sanctity with self-restraint [or discretion]. (NASB)

Does this verse mean that any professing Christian woman who dies in childbirth is *not* really a woman of faith, love, sanctity, and discretion and is headed for hell?

And, then, I have to ask, what about "godly" women who never have been, are not, and never will be wives or mothers, often through no fault of their own or through choice? Catholic nuns come to mind. They devote their whole lives to "godliness," don't they? Will they be "saved" if they have never borne legitimate children?

Either you believe what the Bible says or you don't. Some Bible students and scholars, however, who can't stomach the literal interpretation of Genesis 2:15, offer two other possible meanings for it:

1. It may refer to women being saved spiritually through the birth (incarnation) of Christ—see the King James Version of verse 15. But wouldn't this apply to both males and females?

2. Other believers offer the suggestion that this verse may speak of godly women who find fulfillment as wives and mothers on earth.

These two alternate meanings seem to stretch lucidity and make me wonder, again, why a perfect God could not have made his thoughts completely clear so everyone could understand what he means in exactly the same way that he meant it. And, again, what about "godly" men? Why aren't the salvation requirements for males, as asked above, and females the same? If they're not the same, then I have to ask, how are men saved? Why make a distinction between female and male believers?

One Christian response might be, "Because the accountabilities for the genders are different." Oh, yeah? Then what about Galatians 3:26–28 (NIV): "You are all sons of God *through faith in Christ Jesus*... There is neither Jew nor Greek, slave nor free, male nor female, for you are all one in Christ Jesus...." (italic emphasis added).

It seems that, according to this verse, faith in Christ Jesus is the only salvation requirement for whichever gender. But remember, too, that the definition of such "faith" is complete trust, confidence, or firm belief *without logical proof*. How, then, can unproven faith be definitive assurance? At this point, it might be wise and educational to see the Bible's own perplexing definition of faith in Hebrews 11:1: "Now faith is the substance of things hoped for, the evidence of things not seen" (KJV). Substance? What substance? Evidence? What evidence?

In my opinion, to reiterate, what Christians often refer to as "faith" or "belief" is actually only fervent "hope." As we all know, one's trust and confidence can be and often is conferred inappropriately. Haven't you ever completely trusted someone who later proved to be untrustworthy? I know I have. "Yes," believers will answer, "but God the Father is different." And I will say, "Prove it."

Thankfulness

Perhaps some Christians need to adjust their prayer attitude in order to be truly happy and in line with the exhortations from the author of 1 Thessalonians:

> Rejoice *always*; *pray without ceasing*; *in everything give thanks*; for this is God's will for you in Christ Jesus. (5:16–18—italic emphasis added)

Notice that the preposition before "everything give thanks" is not "*for*" but "*in*." To the believer, this may make a big difference. I wonder, however, if "rejoicing" and giving thanks "in" the experience of a loved one's debilitating accident or untimely death, the destruction of home and homeland, loss of livelihood, deterioration of health, etc. may be an exercise in obedience rather than heartfelt gratitude. Most of us must face such situations sooner or later. Do those who believe give thanks to an unseen god if not "for" but "in" those terrible times of stress? Some, indeed, may; I simply don't know.

I have heard Christians say of other believers who have died, "At least they're not suffering any longer." At least? Supposedly, if the deceased were indeed Christians, they have gone to a much better place, haven't they? Presently, however, I don't know anyone who is champing at the bit to get to heaven. Sometimes when I've heard the above statement, I'm tempted to respond, depending on the situation, "If possible, would you change places with him [or her or them]?" But, of course, I don't ask this question for I know that mourners simply may feel helpless that they could not prevent the suffering.

A couple of years before my husband himself died, he attended the funeral of a friend he had known in high school. After graduation over fifty years ago, they joined the Air Force together along with two other buddies. This particular man became a farmer after his stint in the armed services. He died in the year 2006 on his own land as a result of a freak accident. While working in a shed, a stack of hay bales weighing about 1,500 pounds fell on him. He suffocated when he was knocked to the ground.

At the well-attended funeral, understandably there wasn't much rejoicing or giving of thanks "for" or "in" that tragedy, which left a wife, children, other relatives, and friends bereft of a gentle man's companionship forever. On the other hand, perhaps most of them strove to assuage their grief by convincing themselves that his soul wafted off to a beautiful heavenly abode somewhere. But I can say also with sincerity and absolutely no facetiousness that "at least" he is not suffering now and never will again simply because he "is" no longer.

I've seen football players kneel in the end zone after making a touchdown. Some cross themselves. I suppose they're thanking a god for helping them score—as if any god would give a flip about who scores, wins, or loses a game of any sort. But I've never seen team members kneel in prayer on the field after they lose. If they are true believers, shouldn't they thank their god "in" their losses?

I truly wonder if any sports figures, armed service personnel, politicians who like to be thought of as "religious," and leaders of so-called Christian nations take 1 Thessalonians 5 to heart. When they lose games or competitions, battles or entire wars, votes and elections, do they "rejoice" and "give thanks" *in* their disappointments and losses, capture by the enemy, or personal sacrifice?

Whether believers win, lose, or draw, according to the Bible, they should give thanks in whatever situation they find themselves. Let's not forget the Vietnam War, Desert Storm, and the Afghanistan and Iraq wars as well as the hostilities between the Palestinians and the Jews of the Holy Land and the tense situations in Iran, Syria, North Korea, India, and Pakistan. Will the killing ever stop? I wonder. I know, however, that I'm thankful neither "for" nor "in" the loss of American or any other lives. I'm devastated by the carnage.

Don't Worry—Be Happy!

As far as I can tell, the main reason that Christians should profess happiness is that—now get this—it is not an option for them. The Bible *commands* them to be happy. In the New Testament book of Philippians 3:1 as well as 1 Thessalonians 5:16–18, God, through the author said to be Paul, tells all of his children to rejoice *always* in the Lord! No matter what happens to them or to their loved ones, Christians are directed to rejoice and be happy.

This mandatory happiness entails salvation through Jesus' death on the cross for them because of their sins and his subsequent, unsubstantiated resurrection from the grave. They're taught that he laid down his perfect life for dirty, rotten sinners even though they themselves deserved to die. But, according to most Christian believers, the majority of the world's population is going to hell anyway, despite the sacrifice that Jesus made. Apparently, he suffered and died in vain for those who die in disbelief or "un-Christianized."

When I was a sincere, practicing Christian, I could never get over a feeling of guilt about what I thought Jesus did for me. The sense of fairness was simply not there. My happiness, therefore, was diminished because I believed my sins had caused the crucifixion of a perfect savior. My happiness as a Christian, therefore, was not complete. I couldn't shake off my guilt.

Even if they lose family, friends, and home and face death themselves, Christians are told that they need never feel alone nor forsaken. Scriptures from Deuteronomy 31:6,8, Joshua 1:5, and Hebrews 13:5–6 are cited as "proof" of this point. Yet believers rarely mention what Jesus, the perfect Son of God himself, apparently wailed from the cross:

> About the ninth hour, Jesus cried out with a loud voice, saying "…
> My God, My God, why have you forsaken Me?" (Matt. 27:46—NASB)

I've heard the ludicrous Christian explanation that this was the "human" part of Jesus speaking, not the "God" part. Personally, I need to know through action, not just through conjured-up faith in words from a book, that someone or some spirit being cares for me and will never, under any circumstances, forsake me. I need tangible evidence; and perhaps, if Jesus was an actual historical man, so did he. Did he lose faith for a moment, and isn't faithlessness a sin?

Christians, then, may point out that according to the account of the crucifixion in Luke 23:34, Jesus said, "Father, forgive them, for they do not know what they are doing" (NIV and NASB). But do these same believers realize that some early manuscripts do not have this sentence? So, which manuscripts are authentic?

If you're not afraid of having nightmares, be sure to read the twenty-fourth and twenty-fifth chapters of Matthew in the New Testament. Then determine how "happy" anyone will be during the alleged "end time" right before the prophesied second coming of Christ. Supposedly, even some believers will fall away because of the horrible conditions portrayed so graphically by Jesus. I wonder if it will be because those Christians will find it impossible to rejoice "in" this devastation. I'm happy that I don't believe in supernatural horror stories.

According to some branches of science, natural phenomena or manmade world wars, not a spirit entity in the sky, may wipe out the earth and all its inhabitants in the future. Drastic measures, we're warned, are needed very soon to prevent at least some of these things from happening or to find means of physical escape. Because prospects don't look very encouraging, I'm not at all happy about that.

But Is It Possible for Religious Believers and Nonbelievers to Get Along?

If such values as honesty, respect, and compassion are agreed upon or at least recognized as necessities by individuals, couples, and even nations, I believe the answer to the above question is, "Yes, it is possible to coexist in peaceful harmony despite religious differences." Much of humanity has learned from experience through the ages that these values can be effective for achieving goal unity, but it takes work and steadfast resolve. As an illustration, I'll use my own marriage.

If one partner (me) becomes an unbeliever after marriage, the inherent struggles that come from living under two different approaches to life become vividly apparent. During the beginning years of my research and investigation into other religions, I would tell my husband what I'd been reading. I remember saying to Fred that I thought the Buddhists had an interesting take on life, and Fred agreed with me that their teaching that you do life over until you get it right was indeed interesting. I also told him later on that I thought I might be a deist, as I didn't see that any god was taking a personal interest in humanity's gigantic problems.

"Well, you know, honey," Fred said, "God is far above our understanding. He has a plan, and you can be sure that even when it looks as if he doesn't care, we simply have to trust him. It's a matter of faith."

But faith became less and less logical to me. I required that answers to hard questions be based on fact and truth—not simple faith which, repeated several times in this book, is nothing more than firm belief without logical proof. In other words, faith is only intense hope. So, in the beginning of my gradual Christian de-conversion, I thought my husband, a well-read, intelligent man who had studied German, Latin, Greek, and Hebrew languages, would be just as fascinated as I was by what I was learning. I was wrong. Fred was not fascinated; he was not happy with my new "philosophy." As a result, we did have a few heated discussions until I learned not to badger him over controversial subjects.

Unbelievers can love and respect others just as much as we ever did before we became atheists or agnostics. But sometimes it takes a bit more effort when we're so often misunderstood. A great deal of tact and a careful choice of words are needed to convince, especially those we dearly love, that we have not rejected them personally but only their religion.

I know that my late husband loved me and was fearful of what would happen to me after death. He didn't want me to suffer. I'm sure he prayed for me daily. I appreciated his concern, however misplaced I think it was. Perhaps Fred was an unusually kind, thoughtful Christian; he stated on more than one occasion that I am entitled to my beliefs just as he was entitled to his. Fred knew that I was sincere and rejected religion as a result of much study and research. He knew that it was not bitterness, anger, or rebellion that turned me from Christianity to unbelief.

Other Examples of Diverse Beliefs in Marriage

Dr. Bart D. Ehrman, in his book *God's Problem: How the Bible Fails to Answer Our Most Important Question—Why We Suffer*, admits that he has lost his faith and no longer considers himself a Christian. His wife, Sarah, however, is a distinguished professor of medieval English literature and a committed, active Christian in the Episcopal Church. Dr. Ehrman states that the problems of suffering that he wrestles with are not problems for Sarah.

He goes on to say that only on rare occasions does he go to church, usually when Sarah very much wants him to go. He describes an occasion when he was in church with Sarah on Christmas Eve while visiting her agnostic brother Simon in England. "Sarah had wanted to attend the midnight service at the local Anglican church," he recalls, "and Simon and I—who both respect her religious views—agreed to go with her."

He then states that the service was emotional, but not in the way he had expected. "What moved me most," he writes, "...was the congregational prayer...written for the occasion, spoken loudly and clearly by a layperson standing in the aisle, his voice filling the vast space of the cavernous church... 'You came into the darkness and made a difference,' he said. 'Come into the darkness again.'"

Dr. Ehrman writes that this "brought tears to my eyes...But these were not tears of joy. They were tears of frustration. If God had come into the darkness with the advent of the Christ child, bringing salvation to the world, why is the world in such a state? Why doesn't he enter into the darkness again? Where is the presence of God in this world of pain and misery? Why is the darkness so overwhelming?"

I understand Bart Ehrman's lament, for I have the same questions. But like his Christian wife, Sarah, my husband, Fred, did not. Yet the Ehrmans, so far, seem to have a good marriage just as my husband and I for the most part did.

Another couple in a successful "mixed" marriage of believer and unbeliever was Charles and Emma Darwin. Considered the "father of the evolution theory," Darwin called himself an agnostic. His wife

Emma, however, was a Christian when she married Charles and remained so until her death at the age of eighty-eight. Darwin lived to be seventy-three years old. Bonds of real affection linked Emma and Charles throughout their lives together. Yet troubling issues surfaced in the early years of their marriage. Darwin's growing skepticism about religion caused Emma great pain, which in turn caused her husband deep sadness. And that to some degree describes my own marriage.

Back to the Original Question

I am definitely not a "Pollyanna," but I am a firm believer in treating others the way I wish to be treated—or at least trying to do so. This variation of the Golden Rule is not an original Jesus statement. It is a very ancient code that actually predates Christianity. A truism found in just about every religion and philosophy in the world, it is not a rule of law from any god. In my opinion, it is based on human experience.

So I need to ask again, "Is it possible for religious believers and nonbelievers to get along?" If believer-unbeliever fellowship exists between married couples and personal friends, could it be accomplished on a larger scale, perhaps even worldwide? I don't know with certainty, but I don't think it's absolutely *im*possible. It would take a lot of courage and thoughtful, kind consideration toward those who do not agree with us religiously, philosophically, or politically. Honesty, respect, and compassion in all our relationships would greatly increase our chances for global cooperation.

3

The Omni-God

Most believers say that their god knows everything. Not only is he omniscient (possessing all knowledge about all things), but also, they will contend, omni-benevolent (absolutely good), omnipotent (all-powerful), and omnipresent (everywhere at the same time). Yet, myriad evil actions are perpetrated in this world daily by and on individuals, many of whom profess to be believers in one god or another. Some who commit atrocities even go so far as to say they are doing these things in the name of their god.

Why Does God Do Nothing?

Via television reports beamed around the globe, we've witnessed religious conflagration suicides in political protests. For those who preach passive resistance, I wonder how they justify the violence inflicted on themselves.

And consider the many suicide missions of hard-core religionists who think they have the blessing of a god as well as their families for murdering themselves and hundreds and hundreds of others. Don't forget the Japanese kamikaze pilots in World War II. These kamikazes believed at that time that the Japanese emperor was a god, and they sacrificed themselves and their enemies in his name. After this war, Hirohito kept his status as emperor but was forced to disavow the previous claims of being "*arahitogami*," that is, a living god, in World War II.

The September 11, 2001, acts of terror in the United States of America are something the world, especially those of us here in the United States, will never forget. Religious suicide bombers in the Middle East continue horrible, almost daily, murderous activities in the name of their god. And what do any of these senseless acts accomplish? They create fear, anger, and despair. They blatantly destroy life and property—all in hopes of, first, gaining a fantasy paradise for themselves, and second, providing physical control by the cowards who persuade them to give up their own lives and take the lives of others. They, too, just as Christians do, have "faith" in their god.

As America and its allies pull troops out of Iraq, will it indeed establish democratic peace for the people of that country and its neighbors? Or will religious differences pull the citizens of this nation farther apart than they have ever been?

Then there are priests, preachers, and other church workers around this globe who ravage children of their congregations with disgusting sexual offenses. Adult children mistreat their parents. Caregivers in nursing homes and other facilities abuse the elderly and helpless. Parents rape and murder their own sons and daughters.

Some armed forces members torture prisoners of war, never seriously considering that "what goes around, comes around" when their own troops are captured by the enemy. Some uniformed individuals in occupied foreign territory commit horrible atrocities against the residents that have nothing to do with winning wars, whether the cause is legitimate or not. We've all heard of members of city, county, or state police forces who overstep their authority simply because their limited power goes to their heads and swells their egos.

U.S. citizens cheat on their income tax forms. Even Christians renege on their marital vows to remain faithful to one another until death parts them because they can't control their lust for others even, I suppose, with the help of their God. Factories, oil refinery tankers, and mega-farms poison the soil and pollute the air we breathe, the waters of the world, and the coasts of our nations with toxic material. Businessmen line their pockets with cash while impoverishing others. American politicians exploit their religious beliefs, whether real or feigned. They may lie and break the law for the purpose of amassing votes and power and getting into or remaining in office. And this is a Christian nation?

On international, national, and small group levels, dope-dealing cartels endanger countless lives with illegal contraband. Religious people participate in genocidal acts against other religious people.

Individuals with warped minds torture animals for the perverted satisfaction of inflicting cruelty on helpless beings. Both government-sponsored and individual hunters and out-and-out poachers worldwide slaughter endangered species for greedy purposes. Macho stalkers with sophisticated equipment kill game, creatures from the water, and fowl of the air for nothing more than the thrill of the kill and the subsequent sick display of trophies. And they call these activities "sport."

Others exterminate herds and packs of living beings in unsportsmanlike ways and then label their activities as necessary thinning of sick or destructive animals. Slaughter of foxes, minks, baby seals, and other creatures takes place because of demands from the fickle fashion industry.

Alaskan wolves are chased to exhaustion from airplanes by aerial gunning teams. They are then directly shot from the planes, or these brave hunters land and shoot the wolves point blank. This is in no way sport but simply cruel target practice.

Baby seals are beaten to death with clubs or shot in the skull and skinned. Even domestic cats and dogs in some countries are clubbed or stomped to death for their fur. Some of these animals are still alive while they're stripped of their beautiful coats. This slaughter is even encouraged by governments.

Unbelievably painful, unnecessary experiments are carried out on caged animals in medical labs and by the cosmetic manufacturers. Food processing plants and huge agricultural enterprises cruelly confine and brutally slaughter animals and fowls on factory farms without regard to the distress and agony they cause sentient beings.

Gang members take lives of other gang members. They terrorize and wreak havoc in cities and towns simply for the purpose of being "top bananas" in their rundown neighborhoods when they could be working toward improving living conditions in those communities. And all these atrocities only scratch the surface—while an omni-god simply watches?

Does God Cause Evil?

I personally do not attribute good or evil to any god. Whole books have been written on the subject of evil, what causes it, and why bad things happen to even good people. Answers from believers wherever they are or however they worship, seldom give comfort to anyone and often suggest a bit of fatalism, i.e. a submission to events as being inevitable because they are the will of a god or gods.

Sometimes Christians either ignore or do not know what Isaiah 45:7 proclaims. According to this verse in the Old Testament, God doesn't just "allow" tragedy; he actually is the cause of bad things that happen. Depending on which Bible translation one might use, *God* forms light and *creates darkness* or causes well-being and *creates calamity* and brings prosperity or *creates disaster* and makes peace or *creates evil*. I doubt that the majority of believers really comprehend that their God, according to "holy" scripture, says he is the architect of *tragedy* and *misfortune* in their lives, not just *joyous events* and *blessings*.

But, do periods of light, prosperity, and peace make up for the overwhelming darkness of accidental or unexpected deaths of loved ones? What about catastrophes such as earthquakes, flooding, blizzards, drought, hurricanes, tsunamis, tornadoes, war, poverty and starvation, terrorism, tyranny, and genocide? Some of these tragedies are constants somewhere in the world at any given time. Do these horrible adversities become any easier to bear if people believe they are actually caused—or "allowed"—by their god or gods?

Despite what their so-called Word of God says, however, most Christians will give credit to their presumed creator for the good things but never indict him for the evil or disasters that occur in life. Even though the God of the Bible clearly states that he creates these things, believers are generally quick to blame Satan or personal and national sin for the bad things that happen to even good people—just as I did when I, too, was a Christian.

In fact, I had a recent conversation with a believer about that verse in Isaiah 45. He pointed out to me that this particular passage does not state that *all* evil is caused by God. Even at the risk of both of us being accused of using the disdained "argument from silence," I emphasized that neither does it say that *all* evil is *not* caused by God. On the other hand, I wonder what this devout Christian would say about the "good—light, well-being, and peace—that are mentioned. If this man's God doesn't cause *all* evil, then does this verse also mean that not *all* good comes from his God? And what about the doxology at the end of Romans 11 in the New Testament:

> …How unsearchable his judgments, and his paths beyond
> tracing out! "Who has known the mind of the Lord? Or who has been
> his counselor?"

"Who has ever given to God that God should repay him?"
For *from* him and *through* him and *to* him are *all* things. To him be the glory forever! Amen. (Rom. 11:33a–36—NIV—italic emphasis added)

This New Testament section of scripture reiterates that no one can completely understand this God, and *all things* would seemingly encompass both good and evil.

And here are a couple more Bible verses that I wish Christians could explain to me without resorting to other *possible* meanings of the word translated "evil." If one simply reads the verses as translated in whatever version, there is no recourse than to conclude that God, if he actually exists, carries out evil.

Amos 3:6 (KJV)—"Shall a trumpet be blown in the city, and the people not be afraid? Shall there be *evil* in a city, and *the Lord hath not done it*?" (Italic emphasis added)

Lamentations 3:31–38 (NIV)—"For men are not cast off by the Lord forever. Though *he brings grief*, he will show compassion, so great is his unfailing love. For he does not *willingly* bring affliction or grief to the children of men…Who can speak and have it happen if the Lord has not decreed it? *Is it not from the mouth of the Most High that both calamities and good things come*?" (Italic emphasis added)

Notice that, according to the book of Lamentations, God apparently goes against his own will at times.

Does God Get Angry?

On the Internet at www.skepticsannotatedbible.com are some interesting observations about the Bible. The one I want to pinpoint at this junction is that God does get angry. How long he stays angry, however, is an indication of one of the Bible's many discrepancies. The scripture verses in the next two sections are all taken from the familiar King James Version. In some instances, God's anger lasts for a short time.

Psalm 30:5—For his anger endureth but a moment.

Jeremiah 3:12—I am merciful, saith the Lord, and I will not keep anger for ever.

Micah 7:18—He retaineth not his anger forever, because he delighteth in mercy.

At other times, God's anger lasts for a very long time; and sometimes it is eternal:

Numbers 32:13—And the Lord's anger was kindled against Israel, and he made them wander in the wilderness for forty years.

Jeremiah 17:4—Ye have kindled a fire in mine anger, which shall burn for ever.

Malachi 1:4—The people against whom the LORD hath indignation for ever.

Matthew 25:41—Depart from me, ye cursed, into everlasting fire, prepared for the devil and his angels.

Some of these Bible verses about God's anger once reminded me of cowboy movies I enjoyed as a child at Saturday afternoon movie matinees. There was most often a good guy in a white hat plagued by the bad guys in black hats. When the good guy finally became fed up with the evil of the bad guys, he blew his top, beat the snot out of them, or shot them dead. And everyone else lived happily ever after. Yes, fairy tales are entertaining! (I wonder if any god wears a white hat. Probably not, for I think gods might prefer golden crowns. See Revelation 14:14.)

The Book of Job

The book of Job in the Old Testament has always intrigued me. When I was a Christian in college, I took a "Survey of the Old Testament" course. This included a study of Job. Rather than answering my questions, however, the instruction I received increased my doubts and concerns about God's love.

Christians usually maintain that some of the bad things that happen are the direct cause of personal sin. Believers may also say that troubles are sometimes brought on by the devil, such as the tragedies in Job's life. I must point out, however, that God himself gave permission to Satan to reek personal havoc on Job who, apparently, had not committed any sin that would warrant such suffering. The Lord allegedly baited Satan and asked, "Have you considered my servant Job? There is no one on earth like him; he is blameless and upright, a man who fears God and shuns evil" (Job 1:8—NIV).

When this is pointed out, a believer's response then might be, "We have to remember that at the conclusion of God's challenge to Satan, Job was greatly blessed." I would then counter with, "Had I been in Job's situation, I don't know that I could ever trust God again not to make another wager with Satan in the future!"

Like a child who can't bring herself to report parental abuse, as a Christian I was afraid my heavenly Father would mete out further punishment or that he wouldn't love me any more if I blamed him in any way for my trials. And isn't that the way Job felt?

If any "child of God" was ever abused by him, this ancient story (or dramatic play, as some scholars believe it is) quite graphically depicts parental abuse. Job was severely frightened of his creator—and rightly so. God, as stated before, had given permission to the devil to take from this seemingly righteous man: children, home, wealth, and health—practically everything except life itself—and this, apparently, was simply to prove to the devil that the man would remain faithful. All this parley between God and Satan was unbeknownst to Job. In fact, God never did reveal to his servant Job why he was subjected to such horrendous suffering. It seems, however, that he simply wanted to prove a point to one of his created beings. Notice what poor Job says:

> [God] carries out his decree against me, and *many such plans he still has in store.* That is why *I am terrified* before him; when I think of all this, *I fear him.* God has made my heart faint; *the Almighty has terrified me* (Job 23:13b–16—NIV—italic emphasis added).

In chapters 38–41 of the book of Job, the great creator finally confronts Job. He castigates him, in essence, for questioning his Maker over the anguish he experienced and for truthfully maintaining his righteousness. Then, finally, Job's God boasts of his ingenious powers of creativity.

Without ever revealing the reason for the agony heaped on Job through the devil, God simply tells the man, in so many words (actually, a great many words), that what the creator of all things does is not anybody's business because he is in charge! Job, then, apologizes to God and repents. Of what, I don't know—perhaps because he "thought" he understood God but really didn't? (See Job 42:5–6.) Anyway, Job raises no further objections regarding his treatment and accepts the additional blessings. What else could he do?

Then the creator bores in on Job's three friends who either tried to comfort or give advice to the poor man during his ordeal. God rakes them over the coals and demands that they offer animal sacrifices because they have not spoken of God rightly. In addition, God accepts Job's prayer on behalf of his friends and does not deal with them according to their "folly." (See Job 42:7–9.)

Since I now believe the story of Job, and in fact the entire Bible, is a work of fiction, believers and I would be unable to come to a consensus with regard to the meaning of this ancient Old Testament scroll. Even if it were true that Job came out on top at the end, it still doesn't let God off the hook—if He is truly omnipotent and knew that Job would remain faithful through the ordeal.

If God has the power to veto the devil's evil desires but doesn't and simply "allows" bad things to happen, why should I put my trust in him? This seems to fly in the face of the basic Christian teaching that God is omni-benevolent, "all good."

When I was a believer, I tried never to blame God for any of my troubles. I thought, as do most Christians, they sometimes come upon us because we are not obedient to God; and at other times he *allows* Satan's intrusion into our lives for the purpose of teaching us valuable lessons we might not learn otherwise. One of my college professors suggested that Job may have had to suffer because he needed to learn humility. But even God said that his servant Job was perfect and upright, that he feared God and hated evil.

In my Christian days, I didn't like myself very much. When life threw me a curve, I felt guilty. And, like Job, I didn't always know what the heck was going on and why I was being "punished." I prayed and begged God for forgiveness of whatever sin I might have committed.

What a pathetic creature I became in my Christian efforts aimed at pleasing the God of the Bible and becoming perfect! Since that time, I have learned a most valuable lesson: Love for oneself is the first step toward truly loving others. And this is a freeing experience!

4

This, Too, Shall Pass

Today, as an unbeliever, I am less often disheartened and stressed in my personal life than I was as a Christian. Oh, yes, I still make mistakes and try to correct them if at all possible. I still mourn the deaths of people I love. I still occasionally experience frustration, even disenchantment, with others; but I deal with conflict better now than when I was a believer. I also lose courage and confidence in myself less often that I once did.

Why? Simply because I know that I am not a dirty, rotten sinner. This may sound terribly arrogant to many. I assure you, however, that I'm certainly not "perfect" by anyone's standards (at times, not even my own). And I don't even try to be, for standards differ from circumstance to circumstance, from individual to individual, from nation to nation, and especially from religion to religion.

These days I don't blame myself for every little thing that goes wrong in my life as I did when I was a believer. Now, whether it is a trial brought about through natural phenomena, misjudgment on my part, anger and deceit directed toward me personally, or even hurt or irritation that I allow others to cause me, I have learned that there is one constant in life: Time, not alone but coupled with acceptance, truly is a great healer; and everything eventually changes. In one way or another, whatever my trial happens to be, *this, too, shall pass.*

Maybe not all circumstances that cause disruptions or disturbances in my life totally change or go away. But, inevitably, if I redirect my attitude toward, feelings about, and responses to problems, situations improve so that I can deal with them rationally.

Learning Must Never Cease

In this world and the entire universe, there is so very much that we don't understand. I doubt that anyone will ever know absolutely everything about anything—especially the whys. In some cases there may not be an answer to "why." Some things simply are because of the way natural laws operate. And we, no doubt, are yet unaware of many natural occurrences that impact our universe. Expanding my knowledge and seeking understanding about those things that directly and obviously affect my life are important to me.

I for one have shut the door on accepting anything that anyone proclaims as absolute truth without objective proof. And sometimes my current education is insufficient or I lack the wisdom for discerning that the proof I'm presented may or may not be legitimate. That's why I often postpone making a decision about what I believe, especially concerning religious, scientific, and political matters, until I have investigated the subject as thoroughly as I possibly can. And even when I do come to a conclusion, I reserve the right to change my mind later. I'm never ashamed to say, "I don't know" or "I was wrong."

Knowledge and intellectual growth include developing skills in research, admitting misconceptions, and accepting others for who and where they are on their personal journeys through life. My atheistic viewpoints and conclusions have evolved over years through ongoing investigation, contemplation, and experience. It is my desire that personal research and study never cease as long as my brain functions.

What Does God Really Want?

In the last book of the Christian Bible regarding the end time, a man called John the Revelator tells about his alleged vision of the angel with "the eternal gospel." (The Greek word translated "gospel" means "good news" or more precisely, "good message.") Notice what this John wrote:

> And he [the angel] said with a loud voice, "Fear God, and give Him glory, because the hour of His judgment has come...." (Rev. 14:7—NASB)

Read the remainder of that chapter and the next few chapters, which describe what that hour of God's judgment and wrath supposedly will mean for the earth and its inhabitants keeping in mind, again, that this is said to be "good news." These descriptions are not pretty. They are not things I would want little children to read any more than I would want them to see Mel Gibson's *The Passion of the Christ*, a deeply upsetting and extremely violent movie that portrays graphic brutality, bloody torture and cruelty that human beings devised and used against other human beings.

But most of the book of Revelation, to me, is even more disturbing. It describes the terrible anger of a powerful God directed toward puny human beings who have supposedly offended or sinned against him. Just like he did in Noah's flood, he will punish his own creation including, apparently, children, infants, and embryos growing in their mothers' wombs. Except this time, God's wrath will not entail drowning. Instead, there will be blood-filled rivers and seas, burning of flesh with fire from the heat of the sun, powerful earthquakes never before experienced on the earth, fatal epidemic diseases, mourning, and famine.

John's Revelation further warns that anyone who worships "the beast and his image" and receives a mark on his forehead or on his hand will experience the wrath of God and "be tormented with fire and brimstone *in the presence of the holy angels and...the Lamb*" (14:10—italic emphasis added).

I wonder if Jesus the Lamb and the "holy" angels will enjoy this spectacle as some Roman emperors apparently did when Christians, we have been told, were thrown to the lions. (By the way, it's not even made clear what the beast, his image, and the mark are; but there are plenty of different denominational opinions about them.)

In chapter 11, we're introduced to the Two Witnesses. And how many speculations have we heard over the years about who those illustrious two might be? After they're killed and then resurrected by God, they're taken into heaven in a cloud.

> ...And in that hour there was a great earthquake, and a tenth of the city fell; seven thousand people were killed in the earthquake, and the rest were terrified and gave glory to the God of heaven. (Rev. 11:13)

Notice that fear, not love, is the motivating factor in this "conversion"—but maybe you have to start somewhere. Nevertheless I find all this inconceivable that a *loving* and *forgiving* God would carry out such torment. I wonder, then, if this God really wants love from his creation or simply abject fear like so many past human dictators wanted and current tyrants still maintain over their country's population.

"Feel-Good" Religion

We all want to feel better about the horrible things that occur in life, don't we? Some people simply want to deny them, such as those who perversely deny that the Holocaust of World War II ever took place. Others continue to make their god or gods in their own image and have him or her act like they think they would if they were god.

If you are at least as old as I am, you will probably remember the old hymn, "We'll Understand It Better." The chorus assures "the saints of God" that they'll understand the hard life they experienced on earth "better by and by" when they're "gathered home" in heaven. Christians are assured that all will be grand and glorious in eternity no matter what they must go through during their physical lives here on earth.

Somehow this doesn't make me feel better. There's just too much suffering in this world right now—and much of it is caused by religionists who teach that they alone have the truth and that there is an omni-God who cares about his followers. Without beating me over the head with their confusing, contradictory, "holy" books and trumpeting theoretical, feel-good religious ideas, I wish someone would show me their indisputable proof that there is now or ever has been a god of love.

The Legacy of All Religion

Early on the morning of Saturday, December 30, 2006, Saddam Hussein was hanged. He joined in death the thousands of victims who were tortured and murdered as a result of his personal orders when he ruthlessly ruled Iraq. This tyrant's long-awaited execution was carried out.

And, yet, I did not rejoice, and I did not mourn. I felt only sadness that a man who was born in the same year as I and died on my forty-second wedding anniversary caused such chaos in the lives of so many and engendered so much fear in the hearts of his own countrymen.

Substantially nothing improved in Iraq as a result of Hussein's life or death. The country is still religiously divided and now virtually destroyed because of its divergent belief systems as well as the meddling in their affairs by Western nations.

Saddam Hussein was of the Sunni, one of the two main branches of Islam. The Sunnis accept the Sunna, a traditional portion of Muslim law based on Muhammad's words or acts, as equal in authority to the Qur'an. The other main branch of Islam is Shia. The Shiites reject the first three Sunni caliphs. (A caliph is the chief Muslim civil and religious ruler regarded as the successor of Muhammad.) They regard Ali as Muhammad's first successor. Ali was Muhammad's cousin and son-in-law.

These Sunni and Shiite differences somehow bring to my mind the different views that Catholics and Protestants hold about Christianity's Holy Bible. The Catholics accept the Apocrypha as inspired works, and the Protestants do not. The Apocrypha are the books included in the Septuagint—a Greek version of the Old Testament said to have been made about 270 B.C. by seventy-two translators—and the Vulgate—the Latin version of the Old Testament prepared mainly by St. Jerome in the late 4th century that are not in the Hebrew Bible.

What ridiculous things religious people argue about! What terrible legacies every religion has bequeathed to its followers. It's not a "yellow brick road" that will lead you to the truth concerning divergent belief systems. It's a blood red highway that takes you back from the present day to the beginning of civilization.

Taking this tortuous journey, you will recall the Catholic-Protestant conflicts in Ireland and their age-old religious hostilities that erupted in 1969. You will relive the 1978 Jonestown, Guyana, mass suicide of the Rev. Jim Jones' followers. You will face the atrocious and superstitious witch burnings in the 1600s on American soil. You will be forced to acknowledge the evils of the Crusades starting in 1095, the Central American Mayan Toltec sacrifices in the 11th through the 16th centuries, the Shiite Muslim assassins of their religious opponents from the 11th to the 13th centuries, the slaughter of Albigenses Christians of Southern France in 1209 at the instigation of Pope Innocent III, and so on, and so on.

James Haught's online article, "Holy Horrors," offers an eye-opening exposé of these religious atrocities of not just Catholic and Protestant Christians, Jews, and Muslims, but Buddhists, Hindus, tribal religions, and much more. You will find this informative article on the Internet at www.infidels.org/library/modern/james_haught/holy.html.

In this article, James Haught reminds us that former President Ronald Reagan "often called religion the world's mightiest force for good, the bedrock of moral order." Haught also quotes George H. W. Bush as saying that religion gives people "the character they need to get through life."

Like Haught, I disagree with those assessments of religion. It is my opinion that religion around the world, if we can learn anything from history, too often gives people the characterless and shameless presumption to torture and take life from any who don't agree with them. In its most benign form of punishment, religion humiliates those it deems opponents or adversaries, especially nonbelievers, and seeks to discredit them however and whenever possible. What a legacy!

Science and Its Warnings

In 2006, a national television program hosted by Elizabeth Vargas discussed possible means that could end the world as we know it. In this documentary, scientists speculated that the earth is in danger. Many theories were advanced, and they're all horrible to contemplate.

We were told that global warning, for example, is a real threat. Former Vice President Al Gore is an outspoken critic of human practices that may be escalating this threat. The ozone layer that protects us by absorbing the sun's ultraviolet radiation could be rapidly thinning. We are warned that modern technology and our dependence on fossil fuel are major culprits. Some researchers feel that it may already be too late to turn the tide. The polar regions and their vast icy territories are melting at an increasing rate, destroying the habitats of numerous animal species, especially the polar bears and penguins, overflowing the oceans, and flooding the coastal lowlands.

The stockpile of nuclear and biological weapons around the globe is already so huge that everything on the planet could be destroyed many times over.

Another speculation is that our earth could be sucked into one of the mysterious black holes swarming around in the universe. And still another is that our sun eventually will burn out and deprive earth's inhabitants of its warmth and life-giving rays to create the ultimate Ice Age.

I wonder if anything can be done to save our little planet. I continue hoping that humanity will lay aside its religious differences, pool its resources, share its scientific knowledge, and find solutions before it's too late. If earth is potentially to become uninhabitable or nonexistent by any of these means, could science find ways to colonize other planets that might be suitable for human life? I doubt that any such attempt could be made if certain fundamentalist religions have anything to say about it. They would proclaim that a god has established glorious salvation for believers and eternal punishment for the unbelievers. More than likely, they would say that any attempt to thwart his plans would be dangerously sinful.

Many such believers are so sure that *their* religion, *their* omni-God, and *their* ideas of a nebulous, heavenly paradise for earth's elect are all the answers they need. Some Christians point to 1 Peter 3:13 and Revelation 21:1 as reasons they're not concerned about this present earth. They're looking for "new heavens [or a new heaven] and a new earth." They're evidently not concerned about the way they die, for you see, they (or their souls) will simply flit off to heaven at death or at the "rapture" or when Jesus returns, depending on the denomination to which they belong. They're not concerned with those "left behind."

If such a pervasive, selfish attitude prohibits science from working its wonders, I fear that we are all doomed. But *this, too, shall pass*—one way or another.

5

Schizophrenic Religion

The term "schizophrenia" is usually applied to individuals. Basically, the word points to a mental disease described as a breakdown in the relation between thoughts, feelings, and actions. It is frequently accompanied by delusions and even retreat from social life.

I have read that there is evidence that certain religious groups *may* have a higher incidence of individual schizophrenia than do other groups. Apparently, according to some researchers who have studied and compared belief systems, Jehovah's Witnesses have a somewhat higher rate of schizophrenia than do members of other churches.

This disorder, according to some statistics, is also more common among cloistered nuns than among active nuns and, more than likely, monks, too. Something about the structured lifestyle provided by conservative religions, or the life of contemplation and reflection found in a monastic life, may appeal to the person whose sense of reality differs from that of people not afflicted with schizophrenia.

Schizophrenic Delusions

In general, religion of every type seems to fit the description of schizophrenia in some ways. The delusions concerning an afterlife of grandeur and splendor for all believers throughout eternity come to mind. And of course, many believers retreat from social life that doesn't totally blend with their belief system.

As an example, I was a part of a legalistic, cult-type religion for many years. Even though members were not strictly forbidden contact with nonmembers, this group taught that social and unnecessary dealings with "outsiders" should be kept to a minimum. The leaders warned that anyone who was not a member of God's "true" church did not and could not have his holy spirit. Such people, they taught, were unbalanced and susceptible to demonic influence. I became wary of even my own unchurched father and especially my orthodox in-laws, who wanted nothing to do with this fringe religion.

Most of my husband's family are still devout members of the recognized denomination which my husband and I later joined about seven years after our cultic involvement. I learned an important personal lesson from both those long, unsatisfying but educational experiences. I discovered a great deal about the doctrinal fallacies inherent in every religious organization, not just cults. I learned without a doubt that there is no such thing as the "true" church of God.

Some schizophrenics claim they have a special ability to communicate with a deity. And isn't that like most church bodies? They say they understand God, and "the truth," better than other churches do.

"Spiritual" versus Merely "Religious"

I am weary of having people tell me, "Oh, I'm not 'religious,' but I am 'spiritual.'" I am also tired of authors and Internet chat-room frequenters writing that "spirituality" is what we need, not "religion." These statements in themselves smack of schizophrenia or, at least, egotistic delusions.

I personally know one preacher in a small Midwest town who somehow became the pastor of a conservative, congregationally ruled church. After the honeymoon was over, the man revealed his true colors. He intimidated and castigated members on many occasions, both in personal contact and from the pulpit, because they balked at the new direction, away from their established beliefs, in which he was taking them.

Everything, I've been told, had to be done his way. He accepted no advice from anyone who did not agree with him. He actually exhibited anger even toward "little old ladies" who quite literally became fearful of him physically. One woman in her 80s apparently had come to him and suggested that he, perhaps, as the pastor of the church, should consider visiting the congregation's shut-ins more often and more regularly. This dedicated church woman did this herself on a consistent basis on her own time and at her own expense. This "man of God," however, exploded emotionally and told her he didn't have time for everything that everyone thought he should be doing. When she tried to leave and escape his tirade, he pushed her back into the chair and yelled, "I'm not finished talking to you yet."

This preacher is a charismatic individual (in the sense of tongues-speaking, not in the sense of being a charming person or having a magnetic personality). He kept his practice of ecstatic utterances a secret from most of the congregants. He knew that such practice was not widely experienced or favored in this particular denomination. He had infiltrated at least two other congregations of the same orthodoxy but in different parts of the country with his strident approach. He was eventually ousted by both churches. Why he didn't simply embrace another denomination more amenable to his personal doctrinal thrust, I don't know.

When he began implying to the Midwest congregation that they might be "religious" but were definitely not "spiritual," some members quietly slipped away. In fact, before this preacher was finally forced out, taking a few members with him, the church had split into two factions—the liberals, who were "spiritual," and the conservatives, who were only "religious." Well, the conservatives won. And now the man has moved on to another church, again of the same denomination, in the western part of the United States. I wonder how long he'll last.

"Spiritual" Experiences

One Saturday morning in October, 2006, I tuned in to hear interviews with atheists Richard Dawkins and Julia Sweeney on National Public Radio. Dawkins is a well known biologist and author of several scientific books as well as research papers. Sweeney is a comedienne best known for her previous androgynous character Pat on *Saturday Night Live* and now her hilarious monologues regarding God.

I found the separate interviews with them quite refreshing. These two intelligent people of different nationalities, backgrounds, and professions expressed why they are no longer Christians and are now out-of-the-closet atheists. They each came to their atheistic conclusions through research and reason that were not based on emotion or faith, or belief without logical proof.

Later in that same program came two other guests who claimed to be "spiritual" as opposed to, I'm assuming, "religious."

One was a young male surfer from the West Coast who tried to explain his "spiritual" experiences while surfing. He also thought there "may" be a universal "consciousness" that could perhaps be some sort of god.

Another "spiritual" person on that program was a female writer who embraced Catholicism. She related that one of her spiritual experiences is spending about an hour a week at church gathered with people who don't think like she does, don't vote like she does, and apparently don't live as she does. She "feels" wonderfully connected to them, however; and this, for her, is very spiritual.

As a past believer struggling to understand the church and God, gatherings with people who didn't think like I did and who didn't seem to be "searching for truth" as I was became more and more frustrating. Now I know that even the "warm fuzzies" that I felt on occasion were never "spiritual" experiences but emotional events because I cared for those people at church. In the ups and downs of physical life, I rejoiced when they rejoiced; I hurt when they hurt. And I still do.

Other things such as the beautiful colors of autumn, a gentle rain on thirsty soil, a silent snowfall clothing bare branches, a full moon over a placid lake awaken my sensibilities and seem almost to take my breath away. Even coming to a satisfactory understanding of a subject I've been studying and wrestling with for a long time elates me. But spiritual experiences? I don't think so; they simply rouse my appreciation for the beauty in much of nature and the human brain's capacity to learn.

Definitions Are Important

Do most people even know what the words religion and spirituality actually mean and whether there is a significant difference? I sincerely doubt it, as those who designate themselves as "spiritual but not religious" seem to have created their own definitions. Without going into the many philosophical explanations, take a look at some dictionary meanings from *The Random House Dictionary of the English Language: The Unabridged Edition* (italic emphasis added throughout):

Religion: "[C]oncern over what exists beyond the visible world...
[operating] through faith or intuition *rather than reason* and generally
including the idea of the existence of a single being, a group of beings,
an external principle, or a transcendent *spiritual* entity that has created
the world, that governs it, that controls its destinies, or that intervenes
occasionally...[T]he idea that ritual, prayer, *spiritual* exercises, certain
principles of everyday conduct, etc., are expedient, due, or *spiritually*
rewarding, or arise naturally out of an inner need as a human response
to the belief in such a being, principle, etc...."

Spirituality: "[T]he quality or fact of being spiritual...*incorporeal*
or immaterial natures ...predominantly spiritual character as shown in
thought, life, etc.... spiritual tendency or tone."

To be honest, the above "spirituality" definition doesn't make sense
to me. My opinion is that no one really understands how to adequately
describe the word since I don't believe "spirituality" exists. Some dictionaries show that "spirituality" is a synonym for "devotion" which is
defined as "enthusiastic attachment or loyalty...; great love" and "religious worship" or "religious fervor." To me, these words simply describe a personality trait or, perhaps, a consuming interest. This makes
more sense to me than a "quality of being spiritual."

Personally, I don't know any being, human or otherwise, who is
"incorporeal," i.e. "pertaining to or characteristic of nonmaterial beings." I also find it quite interesting that "spiritualities," the plural form
of "spirituality," is sometimes used with respect to "property or revenue
of the church or of an ecclesiastic in his official capacity." I hardly think
that money or property belonging to the church or managed by a human priest or clergyman could be considered "incorporeal" or "immaterial." Perhaps they simply mean that such "spiritualities" are respon-
sibilities given to a human being as overseer in the church.

Of course, I'm not religious *or* spiritual; so maybe I just don't understand. But let's continue with two more dictionary definitions:

Religious: "...pertaining to, or concerned with religion: Pious, devout, *godly*...."

Spiritual: "...Of, or pertaining to, or consisting of spirit; incorporeal...of or pertaining to the *spirit* or *soul*, as distinguished from the physical nature...of or pertaining to the spirit as the seat of the moral or *religious* nature...of or pertaining to sacred things or matters; *religious*; devotional; sacred...of or belonging to the church...."

And speaking of the "spirit or soul," I take exception to the claim that people "have" souls. Living human beings, from my point of view, "are" souls, which means we're simply physical, mortal individuals. When the brain stops functioning as the coordinating center of sensation, intellect, and nerve activity; when the lungs gasp and cease bringing in air, and breath escapes our bodies for the final time; when the heart stops pumping blood, we're no longer living souls but dead souls.

Further, with respect to the definitions of the words religious and spiritual, I feel they are intertwined. People who try to separate these definitions, especially those of a "spiritual" bent, may suffer from a form of religious schizophrenia. Do they think they're more devout and reverential than others?

Actually, it seems to me that most religious people would almost unanimously claim for themselves spirituality. I can see how some people, therefore, would be offended by being told, "You're 'religious' but not 'spiritual.'" According to the definitions of the basic words themselves, can you even have so-called spirituality without religion of some sort? What's the big deal anyway?

Part 2

A House Divided

6

The Religious War of Words

I remember a saying from grade school that children sometimes spouted if they were verbally harassed or abused by others:

> Sticks and stones may break my bones,
> but words will never hurt me.

But, you know what? Words can hurt! They're powerful, especially from the mouths of powerful people. Whole religious denominations, for example, have been split or formed over disagreements about the meanings of words in "holy" books.

In the introduction to this book, one of the questions I ask is, "Why are there so many different doctrines on the same subject from the same book?" In whatever religious system we could name, there are wide variations in belief. Since I am most familiar with Christianity, I will focus on that one although I will have something to say about Islam later on. Part 2 of this book briefly discusses some diverse doctrinal teachings derived from the same Holy Bible. The so-called House of God, i.e. the church, is definitely divided in many ways. And these divisions have historically caused discord.

Formative, Normative, and Cultural Doctrines

Studying the Bible for years as a churched layperson, the wife of a Christian minister, and as a non-churched individual, I have discovered many different Christian doctrines concerning the same subject from the Bible. Sometimes these differences revolve around divergent methods of scripture interpretations such as formative, normative, and cultural explanations.

Formative: Denominations that don't approve of "speaking in tongues" in worship services might say this practice in the early church was formative. This "gift" provided a miraculous basis and legitimized the Christian church's establishment and formation, as portrayed in Acts 2. To some believers, the real miracle in that situation involved the ability to speak in actual languages not previously learned, proving that God was behind the gift.

Glossalalia, they might say, was not intended to be used throughout the life of the church. For substantiation, they point to 1 Corinthians 13, where it is stated that the gift of tongues (languages) will cease and many of the other so-called gifts of the spirit will disappear at some time in the future. But even formative interpreters disagree on when that will occur.

The practice of tongues-speaking is often a contention between Christians. Specifically, however, tongues-speaking is only addressed at any length in two New Testament books: the Book of Acts and the first epistle to the Corinthians. But even Paul, the alleged author of the Corinthian letter, does not raise this gift of speaking in tongues to preferred status. He says, "I would like every one of you to speak in tongues, but I would rather have you prophesy. He who prophesies is greater than one who speaks in tongues, unless he interprets, so that the church may be edified" (1 Cor. 14:5).

Whether the speaking in tongues of Acts 2 and that of 1 Corinthians 14 are the same I simply don't know. Could it be that the Acts occurrence referred to actual languages spoken somewhere on earth, but in 1 Corinthians individuals spoke in truly "unknown" tongues that required interpretation? Notice, too, as an aside, that speaking in tongues and the interpretation of tongues are separate gifts. (See 1 Corinthians 12:10.) Apparently, one should not speak in tongues when others are present if they themselves or no one else in attendance have the gift of interpretation.

It should be noted that the books of the Bible are not presented in chronological order with respect to when they were written. The four gospels and the book of Acts are sometimes referred to as the New Testament Pentateuch and are said to have been placed at the beginning, though written later than other books, for distinctive reasons. These reasons were not merely to provide biographies of the man called Jesus but also to show the progression of a so-called Christ message from its Galilee beginning to Jerusalem and then beyond.

Could the first five New Testament books have been placed deliberately in the position of priority to make it appear as though certain practices—such as speaking in tongues—were prescribed or sanctioned by Jesus and/or the early church? Most scholars agree that the New Testament Pentateuch was written sometime after the establishment of the church. For example, the book of 1 Corinthians is usually dated around 55 C.E., while the book of Acts is given a date of 63 C.E., 70 C.E., or even later. That means 1 Corinthians could have been written eight to fifteen years or more before the Acts of the Apostles.

Now let's move on to another "formative" belief. The deaths of Ananias and Saphira after they lied to the Holy Spirit in the person of Peter is recorded in Acts 5. This could also be asserted as proof that this new religion was sanctioned by God. Once established, the creator's confirmation by such killings of insincere Christians were no longer needed. If they were, they're not mentioned in any other New Testament portion of "holy" scripture.

Normative: The basis for this type of scriptural interpretation establishes an unchangeable standard or pattern for believers everywhere and at all times, whether in 55 or 2010 C.E.

For example, in 1 Corinthians 11, normative scripture interpreters believe that the Apostle Paul is addressing proper Christian conduct in two different locations. Verses 3–16, they say, emphasize the male's authority over the female. This includes instruction regarding whether a woman should have a covering on her head while praying or prophesying at home as well as in places of communal worship.

This must be the case, according to some, else Paul would have been contradicting his own instructions in 1 Timothy 2:9–15 where he admonishes females to be quiet and refrain from teaching or exercising authority over men in church.

1 Corinthians 11 is one of the chapters used to prove that "in the Lord" males and females are equal as far as salvation is concerned, but not in home or church responsibility. Another oft used text for this normative doctrine is found in the previously cited scripture verses of Galatians 3:26–28: "You are all sons of God through faith in Christ Jesus, for all of you who were baptized into Christ, have clothed yourselves with Christ. There is neither Jew nor Greek, slave nor free, male nor female, for you are all one in Christ Jesus."

The Bible certainly does teach that "in Christ" there is no difference in how God accepts any believer as his child. Scripture does not, however, make absolutely clear that males and females should or should not have identical roles in the church. If it did, would there be so many opinions?

I find it interesting that, according to NIV Study Bible notes, the gift of prophecy is "a communication of the mind of God imparted to a believer by the Holy Spirit. It may be a prediction...or an indication of the will of God in a given situation...." The point of view of many is that prophesying is quite different from preaching, but neither should be done by a woman in a coed worship setting. Oh, well.

But let's continue with another "normative" doctrinal opinion thought to be binding on all Christians in every age and in every location on earth. It's, again, from 1 Corinthians 11.

The Apostle Paul switches in verse 17, so some say, to a different venue and a different subject. He speaks of the Lord's supper "when you come together *as a church*" (italic emphasis mine), abandoning the previous subjects of prayer and the gift of prophecy exercised privately. He begins by saying, "In the following directives I have no praise for you, for your meetings do more harm than good." His focus then becomes the partaking of communion at a church service in the right spirit and attitude.

Cultural: A number of Christian denominations claim the writing of the New Testament, in fact, the whole Bible, was influenced by cultural conditions at that time. They declare that the restrictions on females in a church setting, for example, were because they generally were not educated. It would have been disruptive for them to teach or ask questions. One of the "cultural" arguments, then, is that women today are most often either sufficiently or highly educated. It is, therefore, appropriate in this day and age for women to teach, pray, and preach in worship assemblies.

Despite the fact that the Apostle Paul does command women in 1 Timothy 2:8–15 and 1 Corinthians 14:34 to be silent and submissive in church settings, the cultural interpreters view these verses as only apostolic accommodations to the culture of his era and are not binding on Christian women today.

I am compelled to ask those favoring the cultural interpretation of their "holy" scriptures, "How far does this extend?" It seems to me that this argument from cultural bias could be used to dismiss anything in the Bible if it does not suit someone's sensibilities in the modern world. Doesn't that pretty much eliminate God's inspiration of the book and his intention of extracting obedience from his disciples, male or female?

Now, I hope you understand that I'm not lobbying for either the formative, normative, or cultural methods of interpreting scripture. I really don't care what any church teaches as long as they stay out of my face and abstain from using unwelcome conversion, coercive, or threatening tactics on me. I simply want readers to be aware of some of the many Christian disagreements with regard to what the Bible teaches.

The real question, then, from my personal perspective, is not whether a doctrine is formative, normative, or cultural. It must be, "Is the Bible really the inerrant Word of God?" And this is a responsibility for everyone to determine for themselves.

Conduct in the Church versus Conduct in Society

Christians, as we've seen, obviously do not agree on the matter of a woman's role in the church. As noted above, some conservative denominations believe that definite restrictions for women in the church are in place for all time. Some women, therefore, do keep quiet in a coed worship setting as far as teaching or preaching are concerned. Neither do they seek authority over their Christian male counterparts in the home. Females of such belief systems probably don't even put up a fuss when they are prohibited from voting on church matters.

I would hope that these same Christian women, as well as Muslim and Hindu women, if they are qualified to do so, would not, because of their gender, be prevented from seeking a powerful political office, heading a corporation, or teaching in a secular university, for these are outside the context of religion. I say this because, in my estimation, the Bible, the Qur'an, and all other "holy" scriptures are simply religious manuals. They concern only traditions within the parameters of particular belief systems.

Often, of course, certain religious practices are exhibited in general society. For example, how one dresses or adorns oneself, what one does or doesn't eat or drink, and which day is observed for worship provide witness to professions of "faith." But these are only outward religious signs or customs. The way one appears externally does not indicate intelligence, wisdom, or education. So-called sacred books, no matter how much we memorize them, cannot legislate inner character or right morals. These are instilled in us through experience with others and learning what works best for peace and tranquility in life. How I wish people who undertake the melding of church and government understood this. And how grateful I am that I no longer structure my life around what the Bible or any religious system teaches concerning female submissiveness.

Feminism

Not too long ago, I participated in a feminist interview conducted by a college student for an assignment in her social studies class. Three of those questions I was asked and subsequently answered are as follows:

Question No. 1: What do you think feminism is, and why do you think this?

My answer in part: Feminism means different things to different people. Feminism, from my point of view, is a necessary support of women's all-encompassing rights in society based on human equality of the sexes aside from gender differences. (And the operative word here is "differences," not inferiority or superiority, not insignificance or value.) Feminism is my concern over and reaction to the inequality with which women historically have been treated in the social, political, and moral arenas of life. I, of course, realize that there have been notable exceptions during the course of history and especially in the current age. Some women have made significant strides, but we females as a whole have many miles to go.

Born in the latter half of the 1930s, I have never known a time when the efforts to achieve certain basic rights for women have not been undermined, criticized, scoffed at, or ignored throughout the world. And, off the top of my head, the many censures of feminism include denial of reproductive rights, contraception, and equal pay for equal work. Sexual harassment, denial of education, and out-and-out oppression as well as severe punishment still continue in many nations on this earth.

Question No. 2: Who are feminists, and what do you base this on?

My answer in part: Women and men, of course, are not separate species; but there are biological differences between us, and not just anatomically. A feminist, to me, is anyone—male or female—who believes that women and men are equal. And, again, by "equal," I mean that all human beings should have the same rights or status including the opportunity for self-expression and pro-tection under secular law independent of their gender. Everyone should be treated fairly and respectfully, regardless of their sex. I base my opinion on my life experience, social conditions, and a limited amount of biological research. Based primarily on experience, I believe that women and men should be partners in the quest for better ways to respect and live peacefully with one another. That would entail being inclusive in our thinking rather than divisive, open-minded rather than uncompromising, and more aware of our differences, similarities, strengths, and weak-nesses. I believe that the human genders are unavoidably inter-twined. We should not be at war with one another.

Question No. 3: Do you believe female subordination exists and, if so, why?

My answer in part: I have done a great deal of study on this subject; but for the sake of brevity, I will simply state at the beginning that I believe religion in general is the primary cause of female subordination or subjugation. For a more complete answer as to why I believe this is true, I would have to delve into prehistoric and ancient history, the goddess religions, the development of monotheism in different cultures and, especially, the male dominance in the Jewish, Christian, and Islamic religions, which has carried over into secular society.

Women have slowly been gaining equal status in recent times here in America and other Western civilizations; but I believe this is in spite of, not because of, religion. Take a look at how long and hard we had to fight even to get the right to vote in political elections here in America. Even though some "liberal" Christian churches have loosened their interpretations of the Bible and now even ordain female ministers, in many more denominations both men and women still strictly interpret the Bible and relegate women to second-class status.

I am no longer a Christian or a member of any religious organization and do not believe the Bible is the Word of God. If I were still a legalistic Christian, however, and believed the Bible to be inerrant, I would not be a feminist! That is because as a Christian woman, I would feel obligated to adhere to the few teachings in "holy" scripture that clearly say I must be subservient to men. As a Christian, I would not pick and choose what I should or should not obey from a book I believed to be God's word. I have proven sufficiently to myself that no god exists and that the Bible is not a message from any spirit being to humankind; therefore, I am [definitely] a feminist.

The whole subject of female subservience in Christianity, from my point of view, is essentially the same as the slavery issue before, during, and after the Civil War. And please be aware that slavery is never condemned by God or Jesus in the Bible (which slave owners vehemently pointed out). But slavery was eventually abolished anyway [and this was a very good thing].

Female subjugation, from the standpoint of the Holy Bible, may never, at least in my lifetime, be declared to be wrong and unlawful as slavery was [by society as a whole]. To reiterate, therefore, I believe religion is the primary reason for female subjugation.

Faith, Grace, and Works

Some Christians in addressing the question about the many different doctrines from the same Bible have said that narrow-minded Christians along with unbelievers don't look at the Bible as a whole book. These more broadminded believers disavow the practice of selecting individual verses or single concepts to prove points, thereby, they say, abusing this Word of God.

Yet, these same Christians who believe the Bible is a complete manual and more than a series of verses will also say that each book of scripture must be placed in its correct historical setting taking into account to whom it was addressed and why. The New Testament book of James, for example, was written primarily to Jewish Christians. Its emphasis, especially Chapter 2, is that believers need to behave correctly, that faith must include deeds.

Other Christians, however, deny that works of any sort are necessary for salvation. They might point to the book of Galatians as an apologetic for the belief that Christians are saved or justified, made right or correct, by faith in Jesus Christ, nothing more and nothing less.

Then there's the book of Ephesians jumbling the salvation concepts of grace, faith, and works together: "It is by grace you have been saved, through faith—and this not from yourselves, it is the gift of God—not by works, so that no one can boast. For we are God's workmanship, created in Christ Jesus to do good works, which God prepared in advance for us to do" (Eph. 2:8–10—NIV).

Grace is said to be the unmerited favor of God. But according to the Christian majority, no human being deserves salvation because of inherent sin. Why, then, would God, if he indeed loves everyone and sent his own son to die for everyone, save some and cast all the rest on a garbage heap or into a fiery pit?

In other words, this supposed God picks and chooses whom he wishes to save by gifting "faith" to them. I wonder *how* the Creator chooses his recipients of faith. By chance lottery? Or does he utilize his omnipotence and his power to look into the future and see who will or won't accept his gift of faith?

And what is meant by the statement that God prepared good works for Christians to perform "in advance." In advance of what? Creation? Salvation? But if he already knew who would or wouldn't follow him, why did he even allow the reprobates to be born? Cannot Almighty God alter the future, or is he bound by his own plan of reward and punishment? Apparently, even those who do good works can't be saved if their God didn't bestow upon them that special gift of faith.

Even a sinner's righteous acts are considered filthy rags in the eyes of God, according to Isaiah 64:2. By the way, these filthy rags refer to the hygienic protection a woman uses during her menstrual period. According to the Old Testament, menstruating females and anyone who touches them at that time of the month are considered unclean. This is a graphic illustration of how even righteous acts of so-called sinners are said to appear to God. Does He simply dismiss the philanthropic activities of such present-day agnostics or atheists as billionaires Bill

Gates and Warren Buffett or the long-deceased Andrew Carnegie? Does God only count the generosity of such philanthropists as John D. Rockefeller, who was apparently a believer, as worthy of praise? If "good" is truly accomplished, why should it matter who does it?

Whose "Proof" Should You Accept?

It would take volumes and volumes (actually, it already has) to cover the many different doctrinal beliefs on the same subject taken from the same Bible. I have culled only two major doctrines of Christianity, besides those already mentioned, to discuss in the remainder of this chapter. I encourage you to investigate these and other divergent beliefs for yourself.

Baptism: Among the denominations that believe baptism is necessary for salvation are the Anglicans, the Apostolics, the Churches and Disciples of Christ, the Church of Jesus Christ of Latter-day Saints (the Mormons), Eastern Orthodox, and Jehovah's Witnesses. Roman Catholics have a little different twist on the necessity of baptism. For them, baptism is the infusion of grace, i.e. the sanctifying power, that starts one on the path "to" salvation.

The Lutherans, like some other Christian denominations, seem to speak out of both sides of their mouths concerning the necessity of baptism. Notice what they teach (italic emphases added):

> *Baptism is necessary* because the Lord instituted it, and commanded that all nations should be baptized... *It is necessary* because it is a means of grace... But *it is not absolutely necessary* in this sense, that without it a person could not obtain grace or faith. While faith, being the only means by which we can accept the grace of God, is absolutely necessary for salvation, *Baptism is not absolutely necessary*, because it is not the only means through which this grace is offered to us...He, who cannot be baptized, but believes the Gospel, will be saved...It is unbelief that

damns. Faith can exist with the lack of Baptism, or of the proper understanding of the *necessity* and the benefit of Baptism, but it cannot exist with the contempt of Baptism. He who rejects Baptism, rejects what Baptism offers…. (Edward W. A. Koehler, "Necessity of Baptism." From *A Summary of Christian Doctrine*, 1951. Page 211.)

Whew! Now that makes perfect sense, doesn't it? (Please forgive my impertinence.)

I think what this Lutheran author means is that baptism is necessary unless, for whatever reason, it's absolutely impossible to be carried out. Then, if you aren't baptized through no fault of your own but *truly* desire it and believe the gospel (I assume this means the teaching of the New Testament Jesus), then that's okay and you can be saved without it. But if you reject baptism even though it's available to you, then you won't be saved.

Even among the groups already mentioned, however, there are different methods of baptism. Some baptize by either immersion or pouring and some by immersion only (although some churches will sprinkle, again, in emergencies). Still others baptize by either sprinkling or pouring. And some churches will baptize by whatever means one requests or is available.

Because of the name of the denomination, I was quite surprised that most Baptists do not believe baptism is necessary for salvation. They apparently teach that baptism is a divine ordinance, a symbolic ritual, and a sign of having already been saved. They teach what's known as "believer baptism." They do not baptize infants as do the Catholics and Lutherans. They perform this ritual on adults only and only by immersion. Some of the churches agreeing with such "believer baptism" are Apostolics, the Churches or Disciples of Christ, Mormons, Jehovah's Witnesses, Pentecostal denominations, and Seventh Day Adventists.

Communion, the Eucharist, or the Lord's Supper: Whatever any particular denominational church calls this ritual—the Lord's Supper, the Eucharist, or communion—it has to do with the rite said to have been instituted by Jesus on the night of his arrest before the crucifixion. It usually includes wine and some sort of bread. There are, however, disagreements over the use of actual wine by those who believe that partaking of any alcoholic beverage in any way or amount is sin. They will use only grape juice. And some churches use only unleavened bread while others believe leavened bread should be the carbohydrate of choice.

From the standpoint of Roman Catholics and many Anglicans, especially in Anglo-Catholic circles, the wafer and wine in the Eucharist, after words of consecration by the priest, actually become the body and blood of Jesus. In that sense, then, don't the communicants actually become cannibals?

And, further, how do they get around these admonitions: Genesis 9:4, "...you must not eat meat that has its lifeblood still in it"; Leviticus 17:14, "...the life of every creature is in its blood...You must not eat the blood of any creature, because the life of every creature is its blood; anyone who eats it must be cut off."

I wonder if anyone has ever tried scientifically testing this transubstantiation of the elements into flesh and blood? I doubt that it would work. They'd probably be told that, after the priestly consecration, the wafer and the wine would actually revert to what they were before consecration if someone else touched them before they were consumed.

Lutherans and some Anglicans do not accept the Catholic doctrine of transubstantiation but believe in a different doctrine known as "consubstantiation." And, of course, they absolutely deny cannibalism in their communion ceremonies.

Yet they do somehow partake of the body and blood of Christ "in, with, and under" the bread and wine. That is, they teach that not only the physical elements of bread and wine are received but also the body and blood of their savior which they refer to as the "real presence."

They believe some sort of change takes place or perhaps better said, an addition to the communal elements is present after consecration. They say, of course, that what actually occurs is truly a "mystery."

One Lutheran pastor I know explained that consubstantiation is "spiritual," not literal. I doubt that Martin Luther, the founder of the denomination, would agree with this "spiritual" interpretation. Luther, more than likely, would not have tolerated in his congregations a merely spiritual opinion for the Eucharist. He did state, though, that he would "permit every man to hold either...view [the transubstantiation or consubstantiation view] as he chooses." Note what Luther wrote concerning "The Sacrament of the Bread":

> "...[W]hen I was delving into scholastic theology, the Cardinal of Cambray gave me food for thought...[H]e argues with great acumen that to hold that real bread and real wine, and not their accidents [outward appearances] only, are present on the altar, is much more probable and requires fewer unnecessary miracles... [A]fter floating in a sea of doubt, [I] at last found rest for my conscience in the above view—namely, that it is real bread and real wine, in which Christ's real flesh and blood are present, not otherwise and not less really...." (From *Works of Martin Luther, Volume II*, pages 188 and 199, published by A. J. Holman Company and General Council Publication Board; Philadelphia, 1916.)

Don't you think that "unnecessary miracles" is an odd expression for a Catholic cardinal to use? Apparently he believed that changing the bread and wine into the actual body and blood of Jesus is less necessary than simply adding the body and blood of Jesus *to* the bread and wine. I don't know about you, but both viewpoints turn my stomach.

Symbolism, memorialism, and Zwinglianism positions regarding the Lord's Supper are held by several protestant denominations including most Baptists as well as the Latter-day Saints. They consider their practice of communion as a sacred memorial of Christ's sacrifice in a symbolic sense only.

The objective reality, pious silence, pneumatic presence, and re-ceptionism views of Holy Communion are a bit similar to the foregoing symbolic position. Nonetheless they do contain variances of belief or practice which would take much explanation. These perspectives are held by churches of the East—the Eastern Orthodox Church; Reformed Christians like Presbyterians; some Methodists; and some Anglicans (primarily the Low Church Reformed Anglicans).

These Christians are unwilling to specify how or even whether the elements metamorphose in substance. At the same time, they reject that communion is merely or strictly symbolic and accept the real "spiritual" presence in the elements. (To confuse this issue more, some also specify that this means the "true body and blood of Jesus Christ" is received. It should be taken only by those who have faith; and hence, it is a "spiritual" communion.) Most of these believers participate in the Lord's Supper because it's commanded. They're blessed because they obey. In other words, don't ask and don't tell what it all means.

There are even denominational differences in the disposal or the disposition of the elements (the bread and wine) that may be left over at the end of communion rites. Some, especially those who believe in consubstantiation (body and blood are received with the bread and wine) or transubstantiation (bread and wine are actually changed into body and blood), would, naturally, be careful about how the leftovers are treated. The consecrators themselves might drink the superfluous wine, or it might be poured on the ground as Christ's blood was, supposedly, "poured out." Some Christians believe the unused bread should be burned, though I haven't discovered the reason for disposal by fire.

All this brings up yet another question about proper disposal of the elements—especially for the Catholics and Lutherans. When does the change in or addition to the elements take place? Is it at consecration by the priest or pastor or at ingestion by the communicant? I would think this would be a consideration as far as the discarding of consecrated bread and wine are concerned. After all, no one would flagrantly dishonor their savior's body and blood, would they? (Aside from eating it, that is.) Of course, those who view the elements as only symbolic don't have that problem. They can store the unused bread and wine for the next communion.

Finally, there are the suspension or *adeipnonism* (meaning "no supper" or "no meal") views of the Quakers and the Salvation Army. They believe partaking of the bread and wine is "suspended" as a religious ritual. It was not intended as a perpetual ordinance, rite, or ceremony. They simply don't participate in the Lord's Supper, perhaps based on the purported words of Jesus in Matthew 26:29: "I tell you, I will not drink of this fruit of the vine from now on until that day when I drink it anew with you in my Father's kingdom" (NIV).

This statement should give all Christians food for thought (pardon the pun). Jesus seems to have known the "blood of the covenant" he offered to his disciples was only symbolic of his death, and the cup contained only wine, i.e. the "fruit of the vine." Otherwise, how could Jesus feed anyone his own flesh and blood while he was still living?

Oh, one more thing to consider about communion. If you plan to participate in the Eucharist (which actually means "Thanksgiving") at a particular church where you are not a bona fide member, make sure you know whether or not they'll accept you as a communicant. Otherwise, you might be embarrassed. Some denominations restrict participation in communion to their own members and sometimes to members of other congregations closely aligned with them in doctrinal practice. This is referred to as "closed communion" or "close communion." Those not in agreement with them, therefore, might be politely escorted away from the "table" of the Lord's Supper.

In other Christian churches, "open communion" is the practice. This means that individuals who are not members of the hosting church are allowed to receive communion. In the United Methodist Church, for example, open communion is referred to as the "Open Table." Some of these churches, however, insist that one must at least be a baptized Christian.

So what's a believer to do? It could be quite a dilemma for those who want to be absolutely correct in the sight of their God on doctrinal issues. Does God really care how communion is practiced as long as one is sincere in her belief?

According to the writer of 1 Corinthians 11:27–30, he does:

> ...[W]hoever eats the bread or drinks the cup of the Lord in an unworthy manner will be guilty of sinning against the body and blood of the Lord. A man ought to examine himself before he eats of the bread and drinks of the cup. For anyone who eats and drinks without recognizing the body of the Lord eats and drinks judgment on himself. That is why many among you are weak and sick, and a number of you have fallen asleep [i.e. died]. (NIV)

The NIV notes on 1 Corinthians 11:28 state that, "A person should test the attitude of his own heart and actions and his awareness of the significance of the Supper, thus making the Supper, under God, a spiritual means of grace."

It seems to me, then, that Christians should take heed about why, whether, how, with whom, and how often they should take communion. Some churches perform this ritual only once a year; others monthly or bimonthly; still others weekly. Catholic priests take it daily. I would think that, for believers, this is serious enough to warrant sober investigation. And remember that every viewpoint can be "proven" *from the Bible.*

To me, whatever one calls it—Holy Communion, the Eucharist, or the Lord's Supper—or however one participates in it, this is one of the most ludicrous doctrines in any segment of the Christian church.

7

The Ten Commandments and the Sabbath Day

Judaism and various Christian denominations do not enumerate the Ten Commandments the same way. Although their versions are similar, there are also significant but subtle differences because of their varying theological positions.

One interesting difference concerns the prohibition of graven images. The Ten Commandments version used by Catholics, Lutherans, and Anglicans buries this in the first commandment, where it is less dogmatic and less apparent. These liturgical denominations, especially the Roman Catholic Church, have obvious problems with the graven image reference because of their innumerable shrines and statues.

But in order to retain *ten* commandments, they have separated the coveting of your neighbor's wife from the coveting of animals, slaves or servants, and houses that belong to your neighbor.

A large contingent of Protestant denominations, however, bring the graven-image commandment into the bright light of day. They make it the second commandment and thereby eliminate having to separate the general prohibition for "coveting" into two commandments.

Another important difference is in the wording of the commandment regarding the Sabbath day.

The Exodus version used by most Protestants states, "Remember the Sabbath day by keeping it holy. Six days you shall labor and do all your work, but the seventh day is a Sabbath to the Lord your God. On it you shall not do any work...For in six days the Lord made the heavens and the earth, the sea, and all that is in them, but he rested on the seventh day...." (Ex. 20:8–12—NIV).

But the Deuteronomy 5 version states, "Observe the Sabbath Day by keeping it holy...Six days you shall labor and do all your work, but the seventh day is a Sabbath to the Lord your God. On it you shall not do any work...Remember that you were slaves in Egypt and that the Lord your God brought you out of there with a mighty hand and an outstretched arm. Therefore the Lord your God has commanded you to observe the Sabbath day" (Deut. 5:12–15—NIV).

This is another example of how the Bible often contradicts itself. Did God give the Sabbath command because he rested on the seventh day or because he brought the Hebrew slaves out of Egypt? Did he begin this apparently massive deliverance from Egypt on the seventh day? Or maybe He simply gave the Hebrews "rest" from their slavery. As in far too many cases, who knows what the Bible means? Whatever the real reason the God of the Old Testament had in mind for Sabbath observance, very few Christians these days actually honor Saturday or Sunday with inactivity.

Which Ten Commandments?

Many may not realize that there is a section in the Old Testament (Exodus 34) that enumerates another set of Ten Commandments given to

Moses by God quite different from those of either Exodus 20 or Deuteronomy 5. And it is important to note that this particular set of rules is the only one *specifically* designated as "the words of the covenant—the Ten Commandments" (Ex. 34:28—NIV).

The Exodus 34 listing apparently was given to Moses after he came down from the mountain the first time. When he witnessed the debauchery of the Israelites in their worship of the golden calf, Moses was so irate he broke the first tablets said to be written by the very finger of God (see Exodus 34:1). Moses then had to return to the mountaintop to receive another set of commandments.

Many verbal gymnastics are performed by Christian scholars assuring believers that the Ten Commandments in Exodus 34 are not the same commandments Moses received the first time by God. They do not acknowledge the Exodus 34:1 instructions from God to Moses:

> Chisel out two stone tablets like the first ones, and I will write on them the words that were on the first tablets, which you broke....

In the Exodus commentary of the *Tyndale Old Testament Commentaries*, R. Alan Cole's waffling around Exodus 34 being the legitimate ten commandments is quite interesting. He states, "...we must not think of these 'terms' [of the covenant] as exhaustive: they are but a brief summary of God's demands."

Other Old Testament experts agree with Cole that they are only a synopsis or summary of what was written on the first tablets. In that light, please note that most of the "commandments" listed in Exodus 34 are not even mentioned in the "Big Ten" of Exodus 20 or Deuteronomy 5. Read them for yourself and decide on your own.

First, God (the Lord) begins in Exodus 34:10 by stating that he is making a covenant with Moses' people. In this preamble, he states that if they obey him, he will drive out all their enemies. He instructs them not to make a treaty with the non-Israelites. He tells them they must break down the pagan altars and destroy the paraphernalia used by those nations in the worship of their gods (Ex. 34:10–13). Then comes a list of ten specific commandments that the Israelites must obey:

Verses 14–16—"Do not worship any other god, for the Lord, whose name is Jealous, is a jealous God…." [He then repeats the prohibition about making treaties with non-Israelites and lists reasons why.]

Verse 17—"Do not make cast idols."

Verse 18 "Celebrate the Feast of Unleavened Bread…Do this at the appointed time in the month of Abib, for in that month you came out of Egypt."

Verses 19–20—"The first offspring of *every womb* belongs to me, including all the firstborn males of your livestock, whether from herd or flock. Redeem the firstborn donkey with a lamb, but if you do not redeem it, break its neck. Redeem all your *firstborn sons*…." (italic emphasis mine)

Verse 21—"Six days you shall labor, but on the seventh day you shall rest…." [Unlike the Exodus 20 and Deuteronomy 5 Ten Commandments, no reason is given for observing the Sabbath.]

Verse 22—"Celebrate the Feast of Weeks with the first fruits of the wheat harvest, and the Feast of Ingathering at the turn of the year."

Verses 23–24—"Three times a year all your men are to appear before the Sovereign Lord, the God of Israel…and no one will covet your land when you go up three times each year to appear before the Lord your God."

Verse 25—"Do not offer the blood of a sacrifice to me along with anything containing yeast, and do not let any of the sacrifice from the Passover Feast remain until morning."

Verse 26a—"Bring the best of the first fruits of your soil to the house of the Lord your God."

Verse 26b—"Do not cook a young goat in its mother's milk."

This prohibition against cooking a young goat in its mother's milk may have been because of a Canaanite pagan ritual, and Israel's God did not want his chosen people to be copycats of non-Israelites when worshiping him.

Now, if the above commands are a synopsis or summary of the so-called original Ten Commandments listed in Exodus 20 or Deuteronomy 5, where do the admonitions regarding honoring parents, not lying, not murdering, not committing adultery, not stealing, and not coveting fit in?

Any possible summary of the Ten Commandments that I can come up with for Exodus 34:14–26 is that of the first four verses of that section of scripture cited above (verses 14–17). Here the God of the Israelites jealously and petulantly guards his right to be the only god ever to be worshipped as stated also in Exodus 20 and Deuteronomy 5. Does the Old Testament God himself believe other gods exist?

Which Sabbath Day?

Whatever version of the Ten Commandments one accepts is only a part of God's supposed covenant of over six hundred laws given to his supposedly chosen people, the Hebrews. Nine of the "big ten" of Exodus 20 and Deuteronomy 5 are reiterated in the New Testament in various places. My apologies to the seventh-day Sabbath keepers, but the fourth commandment (the third commandment, if you're Catholic, Lutheran, or Anglican) concerning the Sabbath Day is not enjoined on Christians—but neither is the first day of the week, which is Sunday.

I suggest that those Christians who are hung up on keeping *any* day of the week as the Sabbath read with an open mind what their own New Testament teaches in Colossians 2:16,17:

> ...no one is to act as your judge in regard to food or drink or in respect to a festival or a new moon or *a Sabbath day*—things which are a mere shadow of what is to come; but the substance belongs to Christ (NASB—italic emphasis mine).

In other words, the New Testament teaches that a specific "day of rest" (the shadow) is no longer important—as I interpret this—because Jesus Christ, apparently, is the "substance" in which believers are to find rest. In fact, Jesus himself supposedly violated the seventh-day Sabbath according to Jewish tradition and claimed extenuating circumstances as reasons for doing so. (See Matt. 12:1–13, Mark 2:23–27, and Luke 6:1–10.)

Take note also that in all versions of the Old Testament commandments, the *seventh* day (from Friday sunset to Saturday sunset) is the "Sabbath Day" and is designated as the day of rest—not Sunday which is the *first* day of the week. Few 21st-century Christians observe the seventh day as the Sabbath. If they worship at all, most worship on Sunday, the first day of the week, even though Jesus himself, according to the New Testament, never told anyone to change the Sabbath to Sunday in honor of his resurrection.

In fact, the Catholic Church admits that it is responsible for the change from Saturday to Sunday. In a pamphlet entitled "Catholicism Speaks," Monsignor Louis Segur states that the observance of Sunday has no foundation in the Bible and that "it was the Catholic church which, by the authority of Jesus Christ, has transferred this rest to Sunday in remembrance of the resurrection of our Lord. Thus the observance of Sunday by the Protestants is the homage they pay, in spite of themselves, to the authority of the Catholic Church."

Are Catholics able to *prove* that they have such authority? And, please, don't quote to me Jesus' alleged statement to Peter which is used to invoke the authority of Papal succession: "I will give you the keys of the kingdom of heaven; whatever you bind on earth will be bound in heaven, and whatever you loose on earth will be loosed in heaven" (Matt. 16:19—Zondervan NIV Study Bible).

Protestants would say this is not carte blanche permission to the Pope (or anyone else) to bind anything upon the church apart from what is stated in the Bible. *They* might say that the kingdom is now unlocked for Gentiles as well as Jews and that Peter was authorized only to *announce* what is right and binding on hearers of the Word.

This is another powerful example of how large segments of Christianity disagree over the meaning of words in their God's "infallible" scripture.

Illegal Displays

However believers structure their versions, the Ten Commandments were originally part of a *Jewish* document. The Jews themselves begin the commandments with "I am the Lord your God who brought you out of the land of Egypt, out of the house of bondage."

When the United States Government allows the display on public property of Ten Commandments without the Jewish preamble, it is choosing a Christian over a Jewish perspective. And when it allows the display of the non-liturgical Protestant list and order of the Commandments (which generally is used) over the liturgical-church list and order, it is choosing one segment of Christianity over another.

All this is a blatant disregard, even the violation, of the Establishment Clause of the First Amendment to the United States Constitution. This states, along with the Free Exercise Clause, that Congress shall make no law respecting an establishment of religion or prohibiting the free exercise thereof. Disallowing religious monuments on public property does not in any way prevent believers from the free exercise of their religion.

Basic interpretations of these clauses have historically maintained that they prohibit the establishment of a national religion by Congress and also prohibit the preference of one religion over another or of religious over nonreligious viewpoints. Every American citizen has the legally protected liberty for privately acknowledging or disavowing the existence of God. It is therefore a violation of the establishment clause to erect a religious monument on government or public property paid for and maintained with taxpayer money.

"We, the people" (religious or not) have the right, indeed the responsibility, to make sure that our government does not show preference for any theological position.

8

Freewill, Open Theism, and Open View of God

This chapter may open a new can of worms for believers. Most Christians probably don't know that there is a big controversy in North American evangelicalism regarding God's nature, his foreknowledge of future events, and the extent of free will in human beings.

The majority of Open Theists (OTs) claim, in essence, that God is *not* omniscient (all-knowing). They teach that the future (except for the end result of his overall plan) is unknowable. God, they seem to be saying, knows only everything that is possible to be known.

Isn't this somewhat like the knowledge of human beings? We can generally know facets of the past and the present, but we cannot know the future with certainty. So why should I put my trust in a spirit being no more knowledgeable than I, a mere mortal? For those who take this "Open View" position, the answer might be because God's wisdom is far superior to ours. He, therefore, knows if he should adjust his plans in light of present circumstances. He knows how, when, and whether to answer our prayers, for example—and OTs are big advocates of prayer.

The future is unknowable because it hasn't happened yet! On the other hand, OTs state that God knows his overall plan will come to fruition, but not exactly *how* or even through whom.

"No, God is not omniscient," OTs avow. "That word isn't even in the Bible." I must point out, however, that none of the "omni" words, including omni-beneficent, meaning "all good," are in the Bible. And neither are the words "trinity," "immortal soul," or "millennial reign"— which most OTs, along with much of Christendom, hold as doctrines.

A Tug of War

When I was a devout Christian, I wondered why God supposedly created the angel that became the Devil. Since God *does*, according to most Christian teachings, know everything, didn't he know that "Lucifer" the angel would become Satan the Devil?

The Freewill/Open Theism advocates say, "Oh, no. God didn't know whether or not Lucifer would behave as he did and become Satan or even whether or not the first man Adam would 'fall' from perfection or how Job, as discussed in a previous chapter, would react to the torture inflicted on him. Otherwise, if God knew then or knows now how people are going to behave beforehand, then humans (or created angels) would not have free will to make their own choices."

Now, to me, that's doublespeak. If God knows how things are going to turn out in the end and has a plan that cannot be obstructed (which the OTs believe), wouldn't he have to know beforehand how things are going to take shape? If he doesn't, then why are there so many prophecies, or foretellings of the future, in the Bible?

Again, however, the OTs seem to think that God has contingency plans for every conceivable thing that could happen so that his ultimate and even, at times, intermediate plans will be fulfilled.

In light of the foregoing, did God have some sort of understudy on tap, someone else ready to act as the savior of humankind if Jesus had been unwilling to go through with the crucifixion? If that had happened, didn't God the Father "jump the gun," so to speak, with his declaration at Jesus' alleged baptism, "You are my Son, whom I love; with you I am well pleased"? (See Mark 1:11 and Luke 3:22.) But, perhaps Jesus' Heavenly Father was simply pleased that Jesus was baptized. After all, according to the OTs, if you follow their line of thinking to the ultimate conclusion, he probably didn't even know that would take place beforehand!

OT believers are big advocates of "free will"; and if God were omniscient, then humans wouldn't have free will. Would they say, then, that Jesus had free will and could have opted out of the salvation plan for mankind? This question includes the centuries-old debate about whether or not Jesus could ever have sinned. There are numerous questions for the OTs and, indeed, all of Christianity that need answers.

Doctrinal "Proof"

OTs and orthodox Christians use a number of Bible verses for proof that God is not all-knowing or that he is, that he changes his mind or that he doesn't, etc. The following are just a few scriptural examples each might use for formulating their differing doctrinal opinions. (All these verses are taken from the NASB version, and all italic emphases are mine.)

God Does Not Know Everything	God Does Know Everything
God doesn't always know how people might sin because he has given them free will:	God does indeed know what people can and will do. Orthodoxy points for "proof," to Psalm 139:
"The Lord was sorry that He had made man on the earth, and He was grieved in His heart" (Gen. 6:6). In Genesis 22:1–12, an angel prevented Abraham from sacrificing his son Isaac to God as he had been instructed. Only then, at that moment, did God know that Abraham feared and would obey him.	"O Lord, You have searched me and known me. You know when I sit down and when I rise up; You understand my thought from afar. You scrutinize my path and my lying down, And are intimately acquainted with all my ways. Even before there is a word on my tongue, Behold, O Lord, You know it all" (vss. 1–4).
"The people of Judah…have built the high places of Topheth, which is in the valley of the son of Hinnom, to burn their sons and daughters in the fire—which I did not command, and it did not come into my mind" (Jer. 7:30,31).	Also, Jeremiah 16:17: "For My eyes are on all their ways; they are not hidden from My face, nor is their iniquity concealed from My eyes."
God changes his mind at times because of prayer. Example: " …Hezekiah became mortally ill. And Isaiah the prophet…came to him and said… "Thus says the Lord, 'Set your house in order, for you shall die and not live….'"	God does not change his mind. Example: "…The Glory of Israel will not lie or change his mind; for He is not a man that He should change His mind." (1 Sam. 15:29).
But Hezekiah prayed, and God sent another message through Isaiah: "…I have heard your prayer, I have seen your tears; behold I will heal you…I will add fifteen years to your life…." (2 Kings 20:1–5).	Orthodoxy claims it is never God who changes, but "man" is the one who changes.

| According to the book *Don't Blame God*, written by three OTs, "… in the temporal [earthly] realm, God is not totally in control of all circumstances." (page 140). For one "proof" they cite 1 Thessalonians 2:18:

"For we wanted to come to you— I, Paul, more than once—and yet Satan hindered us." | Basic Orthodoxy points to Romans 8:27,28 to show that God is always aware and totally in control:

"…He [the Holy Spirit] intercedes for the saints according to the will of God. And we know that God causes all things to work together for good to those who love God, to those who are called according to His purpose." |

Admittedly, I have only skimmed the surface between Open Theism and basic orthodox viewpoints concerning the omniscience of God. If you care to delve into the subject more deeply there are a number of books (see Bibliography for a few titles) and several websites that strive to prove or disprove whether God is all-knowing.

I have found, however, that neither the orthodox Christians nor the Freewill/Open Theism/Open View of God supporters adequately address the other's viewpoints or "proof" texts.

Miscellaneous Other Doctrines

Many other doctrines could be discussed about which denominations disagree. For instance, the Deity of Christ and whether or not Jesus the Son/Savior is truly God. If he is God, then did he become so at physical birth, at the resurrection, or was he God from creation or before creation? And if he was God from the beginning, was he also the Son before he was begotten by the Holy Spirit in the womb of Mary?

Predestination is another biggie over which various churches disagree. Are some humans destined to be saved and all others lost, as many Calvinists teach? What about Unitarianism, which denies the trinity? Or Universalism, which declares that eventually all will be saved? It is a common belief among the Universalists that even Satan the devil and his fallen angels, or demons, will in the end be saved. Are there one, two, three, or even more resurrections? When will they occur? Why will they occur? Even the doctrine of resurrection from the dead is not agreed upon among the different Christian denominations.

Determining which church is the most correct is a mind-boggling experience for those who believe, or at least want to believe. So, good luck, friends, in your search for the truth from the Holy Bible if that's the route you wish to take. It will not be easy. In fact, from experience, I know it is an impossible task.

Part 3

Religious Experience in Perspective

9

Who Can Know God?

Most Christians believe that it is impossible for human beings to understand why God "allows" terrible things to happen in their earthly lives. After all, they assert, his ways are far above mortals and beyond human comprehension. We simply can't understand the superior mind of the Creator.

To me, this is another wimpy explanation for why God sometimes acts on behalf of his children and sometimes doesn't. But how can we love and respect, let alone obey with confidence and without fear, anyone or any god whom we don't know or understand? (Oops; yes, I know, that's where "faith" comes in.)

What Team Does God Favor?

I enjoy watching football on TV. After the 2007 Super Bowl in Florida, I saw and heard Coach Dungy of the winning Indianapolis Colts give God credit for his team's victory over the Chicago Bears. I usually think that teams of any sport win because of a number of factors: They could have had better players, practiced harder, taken advantage of the other team's mistakes, or been more focused. And, perhaps, there were just as many Christians on the Chicago team as there were on the Indianapolis team. So, really, how does God choose (if he indeed does) which team wins and which one loses?

I realize that some, probably most, believers will be offended by my viewpoint. Nevertheless, I don't think that Dungy's Christianity had anything to do with his winning. Having the power of Almighty God on any team's side seems to be an unfair advantage! And shouldn't any god focus on more important matters than sports, such as eliminating bigotry, hunger, poverty, war, and genocide between religious factions? But, of course, I don't understand God. Do you?

Can Faith Bestow Knowledge and Wisdom?

Isaiah 55:8,9 states that "...my [the Lord's] thoughts are not your thoughts, neither are your ways my ways...As the heavens are higher than the earth, so are my ways higher than your ways and my thoughts than your thoughts" (NIV). These verses seem to say that no one can truly know God the way we know others.

Paradoxically, theists might say, countering the Isaiah passage above, that *believers* and only believers, i.e. those who have God's spirit and have accepted the Christ as their savior, are capable of understanding God. For proof, they will quote 1 Corinthians 2:14: "The man without the Spirit does not accept the things that come from the Spirit of God, for they are foolishness to him, and he cannot understand them, because they are spiritually discerned" (NIV).

But how do Christians explain Romans 1:18–20 which states that even wicked and godless individuals *do* know all that "*may be known about God*." Doesn't this indicate that there are some things that no one—neither the wicked, the godless, nor the righteous—can know about him?

Karl Barth was one of the most significant and influential theologians of the 20th century. He emphasizes, in *Church Dogmatics*, II/1, page 437, that the message of the gospel is based "only on the power of God with its self-justifying wisdom" and that the wise are simply those who "accept the Word of the Cross by faith." But remember, once again, that the basic definitions of "faith" are: (1) complete trust or confidence and (2) firm belief, especially without logical proof. And, I must ask, is this wise?

Wisdom, or so it seems to me, is interwoven with experience, knowledge, and practical application, not simple faith. Of course, I realize that one can act on faith and faith alone. I, however, prefer that my life, especially in the realm of religion, be governed primarily through personal experience, legitimate secondhand experience learned from others, and whatever knowledge I can acquire and prove with current information I have at hand. And, yes, sometimes I'm wrong and must change my mind or set aside a previous decision until further knowledge is obtained. I wonder how many believers would say or be willing to do the same thing.

The Experience of Others Brings Knowledge

I've heard people say that we couldn't know joy if we didn't know sadness; we couldn't know fullness if we didn't know emptiness; we couldn't know right if we didn't know wrong. If this is true, however, I wonder why God didn't want Adam and Eve to know about good *and* evil. If they didn't know evil, could they truly understand or appreciate good?

The alleged first couple may have been adults in form and stature, but they were, apparently, like children in understanding. They may not have even known about pain before they ate the forbidden fruit; they may never have experienced hunger in the sense of complete deprivation of food. From the Genesis story, we know that they were quite gullible, since they apparently didn't know that real serpents can't actually engage in human conversation!

Haven't you ever wondered what language Adam, Eve, and the serpent might have used? Could it be the language of angels (I Cor. 13:1)? After all, that is supposedly what Satan, as a fallen angel, spoke. Revelation 12:9 identifies "the serpent" as Satan. And it wasn't until the building of the tower of Babel, long after Adam and Eve's time, that God "confused the language of the whole world" (Gen. 11:1–9—NIV).

Further, Adam and Eve didn't have the experience of other people as a teaching tool. God apparently did not warn Adam and Eve that Satan, in the form of a serpent, was in the Garden of Eden and that they should stay away from this monster. Even human parents warn their little ones not to touch a hot stove, stick their fingers into an electric socket, play with sharp knives and scissors, cross the street without looking both ways, or accept candy, rides, or anything else, including apples, from strangers. And I hope everyone knows that the book of Genesis does not actually say that the forbidden fruit Adam and Eve tasted was an apple.

But if God wanted Adam and Eve to remain as innocent children, why did he place the tree of the knowledge of good *and* evil in the Garden of Eden? And why did he allow the Devil access to their home? The Open Theists might say they had to be tested in order for God to know absolutely if this first couple should remain in Paradise. And I say that they might have passed the test if they had been instructed properly.

I personally don't need the experience of murder, assault, rape, theft, or any of the other evils perpetrated on and by people to know that these things are not good. I see the guilt, shame, suffering, and devastation that result from such acts. Unlike Adam and Eve, I have learned not only from my own experience but from the experience of others. And that brings us to the subject of morality and ethics.

10

Morality, Ethics, and Atheism

Morality is a code of conduct. It can be either "good" or "bad." "Right" morality, from my point of view, is the best path through life, as summed up in the so-called Golden Rule. This axiom is taught in one form or another in every religion and humanistic philosophy of which I am aware. Sad to say, however, the basic principle, in practice, is commonly extended to only those who fundamentally agree about life in general.

The morality that each of us embraces is actually a system of learned behavior we abide by for personal reasons, religious or not. Morality, to some extent, is selfish but necessary in some cases for survival and in others for simple acceptance by others, including a presumed god or gods.

What Is the Source of Morality?

Richard Dawkins, in his books *The Selfish Gene* and *The God Delusion*, does an excellent job of explaining morality in terms of the biological source, including memes, partially defined by Dawkins as "units of cultural inheritance" and genes. Since I am not a philosopher or a scientist as Dawkins is, I can only explain my understanding of morality in terms of human experience. I apologize if my opinions appear presumptuous or brazen. I am certainly not in competition with science and do not disagree with Dawkins' explanations.

My observation throughout life has been that we receive information about morality and ethics through many sources. Before we're old enough to form our own opinions, our parents are generally our first examples, whether good or bad. As we mature, we interact with others outside the family. Then we're impacted by our general society, formal education, various political persuasions, and, of course, whatever religious affiliation we're born into, cling to, reject, or glom onto later. These facets of life continually contribute to our moral standards—or substandard behavior, as the case may be.

By the time we are adults, a certain morality, which is not always "good," is more or less intuitive for most of us. We learn through the process of growing up what works well and what doesn't work well in our human relationships and in our particular circumstances and environments.

Religion, of course, is thought by many to be the basis for morality and ethics. I, however, do not believe that any so-called spiritual creed is a sure foundation for good moral conduct. I agree with what Albert Einstein said in a *New York Times Magazine* article of November 9, 1930:

> A man's ethical behavior should be based effectually on sympathy, education, and social ties and needs; no religious basis is necessary. Man would indeed be in a poor way if he had to be restrained by fear of punishment and hopes of reward after death.

For the most part, I suspect that humankind is "in a poor way" because of all the different examples, religious or not, set before us.

Good moral behavior cannot be dictated. It is learned through personal experience with and by observing the conduct of others. We see the results of what our own actions and those of others produce. And, actually, that's the way immorality, too, is learned and often overcome. Morality is most effectively shown by humanitarian example of what is good and right, not only for ourselves but also for those with whom we interact.

Reasonable and sane people, whether they're believers or unbelievers, ordinarily don't do things to others, especially within their own environmental peer group, that they don't want done to themselves. That's why "temporary insanity" is sometimes an available plea in court cases involving heinous crimes.

Those who do treat others in ways they themselves would not want to be treated are generally abominably egotistic and may hold some type of power over others. They may be cruel or mentally unbalanced or a combination of these flaws. They may have had bad examples set before them throughout life and don't know any other way to live. They need help—or we need protection from them.

Far too many individuals use intimidation control tactics. Among these warped individuals are incompetent parents, abusive spouses, monstrous murderers, molesters, and scaremongers. And let's not forget the ruthless dictators and government heads as well as fanatic religious leaders. Their arrogant mental attitudes are definitely immoral. Their ethics, or personal conduct, are not in sync with the morality code or rules for living to which they want everyone else to adhere.

The religious ones give ridiculous assurances that they have the "ear of god and *know* they're right" in whatever decisions they make. They consider the advice of no one who disagrees with them. In ordinary run-of-the mill egoists, this is pathetic and often laughable. But in powerful national heads of state, strutting gang leaders and their entourages, or self-centered religious kingpins, it is frightening and not the least bit funny.

The Morality of "Live and Let Live"

Few people truly practice "live and let live." That's because this laissez-faire respect for individualism only works well if everyone agrees to it. Let me assure you, however, that when I speak of laissez-faire, I am definitely not suggesting anarchy. We need fair government for an orderly, safe, and respectful society.

If you read my previous book, *Dare to Think for Yourself,* you know that my husband was a devout Christian his entire life, even as he lay suffering and dying from cancer. In our relationship we strove for the "live and let live" approach. This is not because we made a formal pact. It's simply because we both realized (after I came out of the atheistic "closet") that if our marriage were to continue successfully, it was best that we not argue about religion or use conversion (or de-conversion) tactics, however "subtle." Neither of us, for example, left literature lying around in hopes that it would convince the other that the belief we individually held was best.

We discovered that love, respect, and honoring our marriage commitment to one another did not require thinking alike about everything, believing the same way about religion and politics, or even enjoying all the same activities. There was plenty in life about which we did agree that made our relationship enjoyable and worthwhile. We refrained from offending or ridiculing the other's philosophies or points of view.

I believe that my atheism was much harder for my husband to deal with than his Christianity was for me to handle. That's because he believed that I would probably suffer God's severe punishment after death because of my unbelief. But I have no fear of that because, insofar as I can logically ascertain, no one exists in any cognizant form after death. It still makes me sad that my dear husband was afraid for me.

Maybe an effective, expanded laissez-faire approach in government and religion in general could never be successful. But wouldn't it be wonderful if it were possible? There might even be a stunning reversal of hypocrisy in both church and state.

Is Forced Agreement Moral?

Many believers want government legislation that elevates their religion to priority status. Some right-wing Christians want the Bible established as the rule of law; but I don't really think they know what they're asking for. They would have to decide whether they want the Old Testament laws enforced which, among other things, would bind them to strict, seventh-day Sabbath (Saturday) observance and require the stoning of rebellious sons and daughters as well as adulterers and homosexuals.

Or they would have to make a decision to follow the New Testament Jesus who condemns anyone who so much as *looks* at a woman with lust. Jesus also disallows divorce for any reason other than adultery. That would eliminate divorces based on incompatibility or even spousal or child abuse. I think, then, that an awful lot of intentional or planned short-term adultery would take place simply to get out of unbearable, intolerable marital unions.

Those who want the Bible to be the law of the land also would have to consider whether to follow the views of the Apostle Paul who, among other things, forbade women to speak in church or to even cut their hair in a short style. He also looked with disdain on men with long hair. He recommended a celibate, unmarried state, as Paul apparently thought the end of the world (1 Thessalonians 4:13–15) would occur in his lifetime. Of course, he was wrong. (But wait! The Bible is supposed to be inerrant—isn't it?) Many Christians want their crosses, Ten Commandment monoliths, and other religious symbols displayed in public places. Why? Do these things enhance a believer's status? Do they change anybody's mind? If those things are not displayed, do they diminish believers in any way? I must say, they don't; but such in-your-face displays do demean members of other religions and unbelievers.

Too many people display the frightening attitude that if you don't agree with me and my beliefs, then you are not my friend or associate, and I will do all within my power to ruin you. Family members have been ostracized by other family members for rejecting a particular religion. Friends have turned their backs on friends who come to a position of unbelief. In the case of nations, war and genocide have often resulted because of government leaders' blatant religious bigotry.

As I write this chapter, the war in Iraq is still being waged even as America prepares to pull out of the country and leave its protection to the Iraqis. Many thousands have lost their lives. An entire country has been virtually destroyed. Many billions of dollars have been spent. And some leaders in the United States have indicated that they believe the end is not yet in sight. What fuels this continuing struggle? Religion, of course.

Perhaps religion was not the driving force in the beginning of the Iraq War (and I'm really not sure it wasn't), but politics entwined with greed, hatred, and revenge seemingly were the propellants used by so-called *Christian* nations. When the Iraqis saw that America's push for democracy in their country threatened their religious life, the popularity of the United States plummeted.

Every individual should have the freedom to change how or whether they worship. And I agree that democracy works better than plutocracy or theocracy. But who should be the instigators of change in a nation? Shouldn't it be the citizens of the nation itself and not a foreign entity? Is it even possible, however, that Iraq could become once again, or at least in the near future, a viable sovereign nation let alone a real democracy especially with their militant religions vying for control? Of necessity, their energies must now and undoubtedly for some time to come be focused on obtaining clean water, enough food, decent housing with reliable electric power, navigable streets and roadways, physical protection from within and without, and burying their many dead.

Know What You Believe and Why You Believe It

In Christendom, most people believe what their leaders tell them the Bible says and means without checking it for themselves. So, too, I would venture to say, do most believers of other religions, including Muslims with regard to the Qur'an, believe what they are told they should believe.

Anyone of any religion who harbors bigotry toward others not like them or viciously ridicules, hates, and even kills in the name of their god reveals a weak ethical conviction, a vengeful attitude, and selective morality.

May we all one day be delivered from fanatical, hypocritical, immoral religion of every sort that does not encourage us to think for ourselves.

11

The Importance of Evidence

I value evidence. A deficient desire for evidence or "truth," especially in religion, feeds the fires of bigotry. When people cling to unproven beliefs, the absolute worst in character and personality can emerge. Believers often take offense, for example, when their particular brand of religion is challenged—not because they want others to see "the truth," but because they feel threatened.

True believers who rely on faith and not proof want everyone to agree with them because agreement strengthens their position. When they cling to beliefs because of tradition or because of what they have been taught but have not proven for themselves, they embrace irrationality.

Speculation Does Not Equal Evidence

Let's examine another facet of the story of Adam and Eve in the Garden of Eden. In Genesis 2:16–17, we are told that God instructed Adam, "Of every tree of the garden thou mayest freely eat: But of the tree of the knowledge of good and evil, thou shalt not eat of it: for *in the day that thou eatest thereof thou shalt surely die*" (KJV—italic emphasis mine).

There is a big problem with this verse, for neither Adam nor Eve died the very day they ate the fruit from the knowledge-of-good-and-evil tree. Adam, we are told in Genesis, lived 930 years. We are not told how long Eve lived after God kicked her and her spouse out of the Garden of Eden; but she apparently did give birth to Cain, Abel, and Seth. And, unless Adam had sexual intercourse with other women before he died, Eve seems to have given birth to "other sons and daughters" (Gen. 5:4) before her life finally ended.

I've read articles by Christians who try to explain away why the apparent immediate death penalty incurred by Adam and Eve in the Garden of Eden was not carried out. I note just two believer speculations.

First, some Christians argue that when God told Adam and Eve that they would die in the very day they ate of the forbidden fruit, he wasn't kidding. *On that very day* the first couple started down the path to death. And *on that very day* they "began" to die, death having been introduced to every being in the world because of their actions.

Yes, death, according to many Christians, was introduced on the day that Adam and Eve disobeyed God; but for the first couple death did not culminate until years, even centuries, later. We know that every human being since the beginning of time has been born "terminal," although most of us have years of life ahead of us after we emerge from the womb. I'm pretty certain that I won't live as long as Adam is said to have lived, but I have passed the seventieth year mark. According to Psalm 90:10 (an alleged prayer of Moses, who seemed rather depressed when he wrote it) this may be a good average: "The length of our days is seventy years—or eighty if we have the strength …."

A second explanation of this apparent contradiction is God's supposed seven-thousand-year plan for humankind. This is based on Jewish teachings adopted and expanded by some Christians, particularly seventh-day Sabbath keepers. Each day, they tell us, is one thousand years from God's perspective—not twenty-four hours! Adam lived 930 years, thereby dying in that *first* one-thousand-year-long "day" in God's Plan of Salvation, so they say. This then, such believers explain, actually was the very "day" Adam and Eve ate the fruit and died!

This Christian interpretation is established on the belief that the six days of creation and the seventh-day rest represent seven thousand years. In the first six thousand years, man has been allowed to govern himself and to fail. The seventh day of the week symbolizes a thousand-year Sabbath rest. In other words, each day of the creation week represents one thousand years of human existence. Those who embrace such ideas tell us that human life was created about four thousand years before the first coming of Christ, that roughly two thousand years have elapsed since then, and that a thousand years of rest will soon be here.

They put a number of scriptures together to form their doctrine, but they have no real evidence or proof, simply speculation. The derivations of this belief come from Psalm 90:4 and 2 Peter 3:8, where a thousand years in God's sight is said to be *like* a day (not *is* a day). The Bible uses a simile or figure of speech, not an actual equivalent.

The Arrogance of Dogma

Bertrand Russell is another one of my unbelieving heroes. It has been my experience that what he said in the following paragraph from *Why I Am Not a Christian* is right on target:

> I think that some very important virtues are more likely to be found among those who reject religious dogmas than among those who accept them. I think this applies especially to the virtue of truthfulness or intellectual integrity.

He went on to explain that intellectual integrity is "the habit of deciding vexed questions in accordance with the evidence, or leaving them undecided where the evidence is inconclusive."

Kenneth Humphreys, in *Jesus Never Existed*, courageously states:

> An optimistic view [of the future path for Christianity] is that within a generation the scholarly consensus that Jesus "probably" existed will shift to an agreement that the superstar of Christianity "probably" did not exist, and we will see more analysis of the precise manner in which the glorious hero was synthesized from earlier forms...
>
> ...There seems little doubt that [Christianity] will survive the demise of its godman, even though the Church itself will experience seismic upheaval. The new home for the faithful will be the "Christ within," a return to a direct relationship with the Creator and a nurturing of the divine spark within us all...
>
> A pessimistic view is that we stand on the portal of a new Dark Age. A catastrophe of some kind...will once again cast humanity into ignorance and barbarism....

If Humphreys is correct in either his pessimistic or his optimistic assessment, the need for proof and evidence for what we unbelievers hold as true or untrue becomes more and more important. My fear, you see, is not of any god. It is an increasing apprehension of militant god believers who speak "for" a god who cannot speak for himself and whose existence cannot be proven.

In America, within the last few years, we have seen a burgeoning of Christianity in its various forms. But right alongside this growth, with less fanfare, is the developing of an equally sinister "religionless" god concept. Increasing numbers of people are embracing such notions as god *is* all (pantheism) or that god is *in* all including every human being, rock, and bug (panentheism).

Somehow these ideas are just as disturbing to me as Christianity, Islam, Judaism, and all other religions. One reason is that I can at least prove, sufficiently to myself, that the books on which religions are based are not without error or contradictions and, therefore, cannot be from a perfect god. But I cannot dialogue logically with the pantheists or the panentheists simply because they base their beliefs on nothing more than feelings and emotion. They have no holy book that I can show to be deficient. They don't even have a savior whose existence can be disproved from history. They simply establish their philosophies on the way they think or "feel" things are or should be.

Dogma without genuine proof is an arrogant declaration of opinion, whether orthodox, cultic, or metaphysical.

Can There Be God without Religion?

Because I believe that religion almost always stifles doctrinal scrutiny, reading an interview with Sankara Saranam is what convinced me to purchase his book *God Without Religion*. In that persuasive exchange I found that I agree with a few of his points of view. Here is one question he was asked:

> Religious leaders of all denominations claim their particular faith is in possession of the Word of God. Among monotheistic religions, how can there be so many different and contradictory Words of God? How do you view these "direct transmissions" from a deity?

Part of Saranam's answer:

> Calling any scripture the "Word of God" immediately lays the groundwork for prejudice, divisiveness, and even bloodshed, as history has repeatedly demonstrated. Such a claim either depicts God as contradictory, nonsensical, and violent, or implies that God has graced one group of people with the truth while excluding others. Selective interpretations of "sanctified" texts support the ambitions and desires of the interpreters and easily lead to exploitation and persecution of minority groups...Religious texts are like inkblot tests—the myths that

people construct from reading them…[T]hey are artifacts—the words of human beings—and are neither holy nor unholy.

I believe, apparently as does Saranam, that "seekers of truth" need encouragement to draw their own conclusions. I agree with him that religious leaders and their followers many times take harsh, rigid stands on a given subject. Such believers often reveal a limited understanding of or an uncaring attitude for the feelings and situations of others not like them. They snub certain individuals and teach others to do likewise. Those ostracized might be homosexuals, the divorced, women who have been raped or have had children out of wedlock or abortions, or people of different cultures. They might even include the mentally or physically challenged, who might be suspected (in some strict, fundamentalist, religious circles) of being possessed by a demon or demons.

I agree with Saranam that organized religion suppresses questions that need asking. Religious leaders, whether Christian clerics or priests, Jewish rabbis, Hindu gurus, Buddhist holy men, Muslim Sufis—whoever—too often interpret their gods or their "holy" scriptures *for* their followers. This narrows an individual's ability to come to her own personal opinions concerning religion through study, research, and reason.

I myself embrace certain philosophic principles rather conclusively. But I'm willing to listen to positions I haven't considered before if they are offered rationally without belligerence and with what the "offerer" feels is proof. I can be flexible. So, I purchased and read Sankara Saranam's book. Arun Gandhi, grandson of Mohandas Karamchand Gandhi (Mahatma Gandhi), wrote the foreword to *God Without Religion*, which, in my opinion, is the best part of the work. In it, he made some provocative comments:

> Since the identity of God is so inscrutable (if not the best-kept secret in the world) and the philosophy surrounding this power so impen-

etrable, religious leaders of various faiths have defined God in ways that raise more questions than they answer…

…[H]uman beings can only pursue the truth and not "possess" it, as many religious zealots claim to do…[I]f we persist in competing to possess the truth instead of working in unity to pursue it, we are going to face untold grief, and worse, violence.…

History already has demonstrated many times over that Arun Gandhi's observation is true. Every religion's "holy" scripture or faith tenets have created prejudice, divisiveness, and hatred to the point of bloodshed. Almost always, believers of any religion claim a monopoly on virtue and truth concerning almost any subject one can introduce. This can lead to intellectual as well as religious abuse.

Although I understand some of the author's positions, I found that Saranam for the most part is far too metaphoric and metaphysical for me. He defines himself as a "yogi, which is simply someone who looks deeply within." His sometimes confusing "theory of self" is weighed down with such expressions as "the individuated sense of self," "the infinite substance of self," and the "expansive self" or the "larger self" as opposed to the "narrow self" in actions. He expounds on such things as self-determination, self-expansion, self-knowledge, self-sacrifice, and such. He writes that selfless actions are derived "from an identification with the larger self of humanity instead of the narrow self of the individual."

By "the larger self of humanity" I assume that he means we, as human individuals, cannot separate ourselves from humanity as a whole. We, therefore, should not act on behalf of ourselves only but should consider actions that might benefit others as well. And I personally believe we can do this without religion or a god of any sort.

In a nutshell, it seems that Saranam wants to eliminate organized religion—on the surface, not a bad idea. His aim is for everyone to realize that each of us is an "infinite" self, a self-sustaining God. But he offers no proof.

One of the book reviewers on Amazon.com said Saranam promoted "a nonreligious religion," and I concur. The author of *God Without Religion* wants a world without creeds, religious rules, and rituals. And, again, on the surface, those are good things to my way of thinking.

Saranam's book, however, paradoxically does promote a faith system, a religion of his own making. He advocates the expansion of "self" through intense meditation as a tool. But isn't meditation, for many people, a religious ritual? He also advocates formation of discussion groups for the purpose of exploring beliefs. I certainly don't have anything against occasional, friendly discussions. In fact, I enjoy such; but couldn't these groups, as another reviewer pointed out, conceivably lead to yet another organized religion?

From my point of view, *God Without Religion* presents an oxymoron. I can't conceive of belief in any sort of god, whether it is "self" or some spiritual entity outside of self, without practicing some type of intellectually stifling religion, whether or not there is ritual involved. I need evidential proof—not someone's subjective experience—that any religion (or non-religion) is beneficial for me. Sankara Saranam did not sufficiently provide that. And he certainly did not convince me that I am god.

12

The Logic of Unbelief

My unbelief offers a positive, logical vantage point. I see that no man or woman is inherently better than I and that I am not better than anyone else. I try to exhibit this outlook in my life.

I don't insist that everyone become an agnostic, an atheist, a secular humanist, or any other sort of nonbeliever. Convincing those who disagree with me that I am right is not a personal need. I am more secure in my daily lifestyle and unbelieving status than that. If I weren't, I would change; but I'll keep studying, researching, and contemplating the issues of life and existence from all points of view. Would that religionists do the same thing.

The Process of Reason

I believe in the process of reason for discovering truth regarding anything, especially religion. I believe in gathering information from history; from the results of unbiased, scientific research, and from religion comparison. I am convinced at this point that there is no so-called holy book from any perfect, creator god anywhere. Humankind has not been given any absolutely clear instructions without contradiction from a spirit entity or entities about how we are to live or how we are to worship him, her, it, or them.

With that in mind, I suggest that you read David Mills' book, *Atheist Universe*, for his intriguing, straightforward, and well-defined analyses regarding why a god could not have had anything to do with creation. Mills will cause you to think and, perhaps, in one way or another, dislodge you from a fence-sitting position between reason and religious faith.

Dan Barker, in his book *Godless: How an Evangelical Preacher Became One of America's Leading Atheists*, does an excellent job of debunking theism. His honesty about how he gradually separated himself from religious superstition is not only refreshing but inspiring.

I personally have tried to find evidence for god, but so far I have discovered no objective, discernible proof that one ever existed. And, yes, admittedly, *but for reason*, I have found no convincing support with which I could convince any firm believer that a god or gods do *not* exist.

Perhaps honest believers would make a similar statement in that they have found no concrete proof that a god or gods do exist. How sad (and frustrating) that religionists by and large simply base acceptance of a deity on subjective faith in a physical (and contradictory) book dubbed "holy" and interpreted for them by mere humans. In addition, many religious people fear ostracism by family, friends, employers, or neighbors if they abandon an approved belief system. And it is true that in some countries prison, torture, and ultimately death remain legitimate fears for freethinkers. Will it become so in America? I don't know, but all religious fanaticism is a form of terrorism.

Believers see the wonders of the universe and nature and conclude, again without proof, that they could not exist were it not for an Intelligent Designer. They may have encountered what they consider are miracle-type events in their lives. Perhaps they themselves can explain what happened in no other way than God or his angels did it! But these, again, are subjective, distorted conclusions fired by emotion and blind faith. Unexplained events cannot be attributed dogmatically to divine intervention. Ignorance, for either an unbeliever or a believer, is never proof of anything. Things happen.

New "Truth"?

Conviction for nonbelievers is not carved in stone. I, personally, do not have "faith" that any sort of god is nonexistent. I have a commitment to unvarnished truth and objective proof, not to church doctrine or mythical suppositions such as virgin births, resurrection from death, heaven, hell, miracles—all of which can be found in the myths, legends, and folklore throughout the world's religious history. What makes Christian tradition, for example, any more feasible than other antiquated myths, most of which have been abandoned?

Freethinkers are constantly on the alert for better, more complete explanations. The majority of us would willingly change our direction if absolute proof showed that we were incorrect. This is true for legitimate science as well.

Religious leaders also might possibly moderate some of their stances on certain matters, indicating that God has revealed "new truth" to them—such as, perhaps, the declaration from the late Pope John Paul II, reported in various news media back in 1996. This Pope proclaimed that the theory of evolution is "more that just a hypothesis" and has been buttressed by scientific studies and discoveries since Charles Darwin. He, however, maintained that the critical teaching of the Catholic Church is that God infuses souls into man—regardless of what process he might have used to create our physical bodies.

In other words, God may have used the evolutionary process in physical creation. Science, however, the Pope insisted, can never identify for us "the moment of the transition into the spiritual," whatever that means. That, he asserted, is an exclusive matter setting forth magisterium, the official teaching of the Roman Catholic Church. (Isn't that rather like keeping your cake and eating it, too?)

Limbus Patrum and Limbus Infantium

Remember *limbus patrum*? This is the Catholic teaching that people of great faith who lived and died before Jesus' redemptive death and resurrection waited in an intermediate state between heaven and hell. This limbo was expunged when Jesus came to lead all those people to heaven. (No "proof" was ever offered, however.)

Now, the Catholics are getting rid of *limbus infantium*. Apparently, the current Pope Benedict XVI never believed in the idea that limbo existed for unbaptized infants and children. Before his election he was reported to have said: "Personally, I would let it drop, since it has always been only a theological hypothesis."

At one time in the history of the church, under the leadership of St. Augustine of Hippo (354–430 A.D.), the patron saint of brewers because of his conversion from a former life of debauchery, baptism was absolutely necessary for salvation. Even babies would be consigned to hell if they had not been baptized. St. Augustine did, however, concede that once in hell their torment would be the mildest of all punishment.

Then along came St. Thomas Aquinas (1226–1274 A.D.). He was the first major theologian to speculate about limbo as a place on the edge of heaven. There unbaptized babies would exist in a state of "natural happiness" but would not be able to dwell with God.

In 2004, a commission was assigned by Pope John Paul II to look into the matter since the belief that unbaptized children would stay in limbo has never been part of *official* church doctrine. This 2005 commission concluded that God wants all souls to be saved. In effect this now means that all children who die, baptized or not, go directly to heaven at death. A general consensus among the Catholic hierarchy seems to be that purgatory for unbaptized babies *no longer exists*!

No longer exists? At what precise moment was purgatory for babies abolished? If I were a Catholic who had believed in purgatory, I'd wonder if it ever existed at all. Many would call this "spiritual growth." I define it as "convenient conviction" in response to the growing public awareness of legitimate science and dissatisfaction with religion in general.

How I wish I could write best-selling fiction like churches do!

A Tired Old Argument

I have wondered, especially in the last few years, if the majority of religious people believe in a god or gods and what their holy books and revered leaders teach because they are afraid *not* to believe. Perhaps, whether they realize it or not, they agree with the 17th-century French philosopher Blaise Pascal and what is known as "Pascal's wager." Pascal claimed that the eternal good obtained through opting for faith in God is infinitely more rational than not striving for this faith even if objective certainty cannot be obtained. He urged unbelievers to pray, go to church, attend mass (he was a Catholic), and do all that is necessary for development of godly faith.

In other words, those who profess belief in God and who abide by all the rules and tenets of their chosen "faith" haven't lost anything if no god exists. On the other hand, if one chooses belief in God, and it turns out that one really does exist, that individual has gained everything for eternity. I would call that mindset a real copout, and frankly, I'm weary of its use. It's like paying "protection money" to the mafia.

Beliefs based upon what we think will benefit us are neither logical nor honest. Wouldn't you think, for example, that "choosing" a religion or changing church membership so you could marry someone you have come to love and want to marry falls in the same category of false faith and pretense? And wouldn't any god, if one truly exists and is worth his salt, know whether or not an individual is just pretending simply to obtain a desire or to be on the safe side for eternity?

Life Experience, a Process of Evolution

Basically, we humans have learned the little we know about how to live together through a process of evolution—through trial and error. Experience has been our best teacher. Had it not been for the interference of all sorts of religion through the ages, I wonder if our world now might be a happier, healthier place. Perhaps war would be nonexistent or at least less prevalent because we would care for each other without prejudgments concerning religious differences, ethnicity, skin color, gender, sexual orientation, or societal status.

Without religious prejudices, we might have created a worldwide society with little or no homelessness, hunger, or illiteracy. In such a world, we could share peacefully the unique riches of our individual homelands. We could appreciate and not squander or hoard for ourselves the natural resources unique to our part of the planet. Individual nations would not willy-nilly take for themselves riches from other parts of earth, for example, by provoking war under false pretenses. Earth's collective wealth could be used for the benefit of all. Our environment might be less polluted, for we would care more deeply for our physical planet itself rather than the nebulous promise of paradise somewhere beyond.

Without intrusion of various belief systems, we might have wiser government leaders in place. "Fairness for all" would be the watchwords in conducting the policies and affairs of a nation, not individual sanctimonious views about a god and his, her, or its requirements for so-called righteousness.

But what chance is there for the accomplishment of these things? Believers are convinced that a particular god or a pantheon of gods is on their side. They are convinced that all people should convert to their mode of worship or be damned. When most religions claim exclusive "truth" and insist that everyone agree with them, what chance do we have?

Today this competition between diverse religious bodies is combined with the availability of weapons of potential mass destruction. Many of these ultra-dangerous devices are in the hands of sometimes very "religious" warmongers around the globe. This is definitely upsetting to rational thinkers. War and destruction in the name of some god or at the behest of unbalanced world leaders may evolve us all right out of existence. And that is totally illogical.

13

How Tolerant Should We Be?

Some people who have never learned to think for themselves may indeed need a belief system. They may need instruction from others who, they believe, are more educated or spiritual than they. They may think they need moral guidance from those placed on religious pedestals to tell them how they should behave and what they must believe.

Religious tentacles are deeply embedded in the average believer's brain. Some cling to a belief in a god of some sort because of their unrealistic prospects of gaining pie-in-the-sky eternal life and its fabricated rewards. Otherwise, the here-and-now would be hopeless and devoid of all joy and meaning for them. I fear that religious mythology has frozen logic and the reasoning capacity in most people. Even so, there is no excuse for damning others who don't agree with them. This is flagrant intolerance.

Religious Tolerance and Science

In November, 2006, a forum took place at the Salk Institute for Biological Studies in La Jolla, California. Many scientific luminaries, some of believer status but most of them unbelievers, attended. The following are a few quotes from that gathering as reported in newspapers and on various websites:

"The world needs to wake up from its long nightmare of religious belief."—*Steven Weinberg, a Nobel laureate in physics*

"Let's teach our children from a very young age about the story of the universe and its incredible richness and beauty. It is already so much more glorious and awesome—and even comforting—than anything offered by any scripture or God concept I know."—*Carolyn Porco, a senior research scientist at the Space Science Institute in Boulder, Colorado*

"The core of science is not a mathematical model; it is intellectual honesty… Every religion is making claims about the way the world is…There are claims about the divine origin of certain books, about the virgin birth of certain people, about the survival of the human personality after death. These claims purport to be about reality…I don't know how many more engineers and architects need to fly planes into our buildings before we realize that this is not merely a matter of lack of education or economic despair."—*Sam Harris, a doctoral student in neuroscience and a best-selling author*

"There are six billion people in the world…If we think that we are going to persuade them to live a rational life based on scientific knowledge, we are not only dreaming—it is like believing in the fairy godmother…People need to find meaning and purpose in life…I don't think we want to take that away from them."—*Francisco J. Ayala, an evolutionary biologist at the University of California, Irvine, and a former Roman Catholic priest*

"I think we need to respect people's philosophical notions unless those notions are wrong…The earth isn't 6,000 years old…The

Kennewick man was not a Umatilla Indian…Science does not make it impossible to believe in God…We should recognize that fact and live with it and stop being so pompous about it."
—*Lawrence M. Krauss, a physicist at Case Western Reserve University known for his staunch opposition to teaching creationism*

"I am utterly fed up with the respect that we—all of us, including the secular among us—are brainwashed into bestowing on religion…Children are systematically taught that there is a higher kind of knowledge which comes from faith, which comes from revelation, which comes from scripture, which comes from tradition, and that it is the equal if not the superior of knowledge that comes from real evidence."—*Richard Dawkins, Oxford evolutionary biologist and best-selling author*

As you can see from the above quotes, strong feelings were evoked at the Salk Institute forum. None of these scientists are wild-eyed fanatics. They simply have different opinions. Some feel that most believers need their pedestals to elevate their religion and its leaders. Others want all religious pedestals dismantled.

Straw Men

After my first book was published, one of my Lutheran in-laws, a retired minister, made the statement to someone else that I had "created straw men" in my assessment of religion. When I mentioned this to another relative who inquired about the book, she asked me what he meant by "straw men." I explained to her that he most likely felt that I had imagined unreal problems in the Bible.

I don't know that she *didn't* read what I had written, but I doubt that she did, as most orthodox believers really don't like challenges to their "faith." They prefer the comfortable status quo and will take the word of a "frocked" individual over one who has no religious credentials, no matter how many years she has studied the Bible and various belief systems.

I find it quite interesting that this preacher didn't bother approaching me personally about his opinions. And he didn't disprove anything I wrote—at least, as I said, to my face. Other in-laws, some of my own relatives, and friends reacted to my atheism just like many Christians do—with intolerance and/or condescension or, by some, pity.

In his article "Should Atheists Be More Tolerant? Should Atheists Not Criticize Religion?" Austin Cline stated in part:

> When we atheists have the gall to speak out and actually say what we think, a bad situation becomes intolerable...[Most criticizing Christians] don't offer substantive counter-arguments to atheists' critiques of religion and theism because they have none to offer. The best they can do is cry that the critiques shouldn't be raised to begin with [like my in-law's analysis that I had "created straw men"]. They can't say that openly because they recognize it as genuine intolerance, so they try to saddle atheists with fake claims of intolerance in hope of getting them to self-censor. Perhaps [they hope that] others will refuse to pay any attention to atheists' criticisms on the assumption that they are just being mean and intolerant.
>
> This is ethically and intellectually deplorable...If anything, such statements should be seen as a sign that atheistic critiques of religion are starting to afflict the comfortable and discomfit those who had grown used to their positions of intellectual respectability...[I]t's a sign that atheistic critiques of religion are having an impact....

When Tolerance Leads to Chaos

Religionists are notorious for their attention seeking. They do not care that their religious affirmations on currency and in national anthems, oaths, or pledges are affronts to law-abiding patriots who worship a different god or no god. They vie for the "right" to flaunt their activities and display their worship artifacts and belief tenets on public property—no matter that everyone doesn't agree with them. Yet, most believers of whatever religion deny the same privileges they covet to those who have no belief system or worship no god.

An incident that occurred in November 2006 comes to mind as an example of disregard for religions other than one's own. Six Muslim imams were removed from a flight originating at the Minneapolis-St. Paul International Airport. The men were escorted off a Phoenix-bound US Airways flight after a ticket agent and passengers said they were praying loudly at the gate and obtrusively visiting each other while on the plane before takeoff.

These imams, who are leaders of prayer in Islamic mosques, had attended a religious conference in Bloomington, Illinois. They were questioned by the airport authorities and the FBI before they were released. This incident caused a nationwide debate about security concerns versus the imams' civil rights.

Their very loud prayers, apparently, included chanting "Allah, Allah, Allah" before the flight. The imams said that their prayers were standard sunset prayers. In addition, two of them requested seat-belt extenders that an off-duty flight attendant didn't think the men were large enough to need. (According to police reports, the weights of these two Muslims were 230 and 250 pounds.)

Because of the many terrorist attacks by fanatical Islamic believers worldwide and their widespread hatred of all not of their religion, I can't say I would have been unconcerned over the situation. It probably would have crossed my mind that seat-belt extenders could be potential weapons. I might have wondered about other plans they had concocted for that flight. This is one isolated example of how religious practices can produce negative consequences when they ooze into the public arena.

The airline reviewed but did not change its policies in light of that incident. The crew followed procedure and acted out of concern for the safety of others. The six imams involved flew home the next day on another airline. Afterward, however, area Muslim leaders requested a private prayer room at Minneapolis-St. Paul International.

Airports, street corners, public parks, and government buildings are not the exclusive domains of religionists. None of these areas are designed for the promotion of a particular belief system. They are not there for the exercise of ritualistic activities or display of tenets of "faith."

The question, then, still remains: How tolerant should we be?

At times the fact that we unbelievers simply exist is annoying to some religious people. Nevertheless, as far as my personal take on religious tolerance is concerned, I say to every believer, "Go ahead and personally adorn your body with your religious symbols. Go ahead and pray your prayers, preach your sermons, and display your tenets of belief *in appropriate settings* that do not intrude into my personal space; and I promise not to do anything overtly 'atheistic' (whatever that could possibly be) in public arenas. Write your books and editorials for those willing to read them. State your case *sans militancy*. But allow others who don't agree with you the same freedoms of expression without harassment, ridicule, or threats of violence."

14

What's It Going to Take?

If every religion would stop insisting that all adopt the same belief system—theirs—then perhaps peace for the entire world could become reality.

It seems to me that Catholics and Protestants of various persuasions are the most obvious culprits in proselytizing efforts. And, as we've seen, even among themselves they are not in agreement about what the Bible means. Theirs is a religious war of verbal semantics.

All their conversion tactics, therefore, do not impress me in a good sense. They simply make me wonder if god-believers really care about others. Is their religious pushiness simply an exercise in obedience to commands recorded in an ancient book designated as "holy" by mere men? Is it for their own sakes, their own salvation, that Christians feel obligated to go into all the world, preach to every creature, make disciples, and convert all unbelievers—even against the will or desire of those they approach?

Only a Thousand Years of Peace?

Some Christian denominations, based on their literal interpretation of the Bible, teach the coming of a peaceful earthly millennium (a thousand years) after which all hell will break loose when the devil wages war against God's people—the Christians (Revelation 20). But this Satan will be finally defeated, restrained, and tortured for eternity along with his demons, which ostensibly comprise one-third of the angels which God himself created.

In Louis A. Brighton's commentary on the book of Revelation, page 329, he states:

> The dragon sweeps down with his tail "the third of the stars of heaven" (12:4). Stars represent the angels (1:20)…Here in Revelation 12:4, the casting of the stars out of heaven to the earth dramatically portrays the dragon pulling other angels with him in his rebellion against God. A third of the stars were involved with the dragon in this rebellion. Whether one takes "the third" as a literal number or as a symbolic number, it suggests not a majority, but a sizable minority of the angelic host. This is the only reference in the Bible which suggests the number of angels that the dragon took with him in his opposition to God.

Now, to me, this sounds like the basis for an exciting Harry Potter book.

How much better it would be if we could have peace on earth, not for just a thousand years, but for as long as the sun bestows its life-giving rays, nurturing rain keeps our farmlands arable, undefiled air fills our lungs, and planets remain in their orbits.

But is it too late? Are there not enough earthlings to truly care about our little planet and its inhabitants? What chance do we have with so many weapons of mass destruction in the hands of warmongers? If the earth's nations do not worship supernatural gods, they seem to worship human leaders who rule and punish like gods. Have not yet enough false gods and goddesses such as Zeus, Horus, Isis, Osiris, and a horde of others worshiped in antiquity faded out of existence?

My heart aches for those who cling to religious fantasies that falsely assure them of life after death in exchange for submission to an imaginary deity. Their foggy, so-called spiritual eyesight can't focus on the wonderful life they could have in the here-and-now if they actually treated others the way they wish to be treated—or as I prefer to say, "if they actually did *not* treat others the way they themselves do not wish to be treated."

I, Too, Have a Dream

Martin Luther King, Jr. was a Baptist minister who fought courageously for racial equality and against poverty until his assassination in April 1968. But five years before that tragedy, he delivered an eloquent plea that has come to be known as the "I Have a Dream" speech. The day was August 28, 1963, and the location was the steps of the Lincoln Memorial in Washington, D.C. His dream included the hopes that America would:

>...one day rise up and live out the true meaning of its creed: "We hold these truths to be self-evident: that all men are created equal."
>
>...one day on the red hills of Georgia the sons of former slaves and the sons of former slave owners will be able to sit down together at the table of brotherhood.
>
>...one day even the state of Mississippi, a state sweltering with the heat of injustice...the heat of oppression, will be transformed into an oasis of freedom and justice.
>
>...my four little children will one day live in a nation where they will not be judged by the color of their skin but by the content of their character...

...one day, down in Alabama...little black boys and black girls will be able to join hands with little white boys and white girls as sisters and brothers....

Dr. King also on that occasion in 1963 preached some of his religious beliefs with which I, of course, do not agree. I am far more confident, however, that his dream for a racially unbigoted America will come true, for even now a man who is partially of his race is president of our United States. My dream for a religiously unbiased America, on the other hand, may not come true in my lifetime, for Dr. King believed the Bible is God's Word and that a loving, personal God exists, while I do not.

With that in mind, then, I wonder how American citizens would react if instead of swearing on the Bible on inauguration day, as has become the custom, a president-elect would place his hand on the Constitution of the United States and promise to uphold that document. After all, America is a religiously pluralistic society.

I would hope that Dr. King, a valiant man, would have respected me despite our differences, just as I still honor his memory because of our agreements. As Richard Carrier, a fellow nonbeliever and prolific writer, has said, "It is better to be good to each other and to build on what we all agree to be true than to insist that we all think alike."

My dream includes Dr. King's secular hopes for America; but it goes far beyond those. I have a dream that one day my freedom *from* religion as well as another's freedom *of* religion will be respected. My dream is that believers and unbelievers alike will judge all others, not on their affiliation with a religious body, but, to borrow words from Dr. King, on "the content of their character." My dream is that people will elect leaders because of their abilities to govern fairly, their desire to keep America free—not because of their religious or nonreligious beliefs.

American tax-supported representatives are ostensibly in office for the purpose of ensuring life, liberty, and the pursuit of happiness for all law-abiding citizens, not just religious people and not just the majority. How or whether someone worships should not be determined by any civil or faith-based institution. Government should stay out of religion altogether. It should concentrate on the overall physical problems of feeding, housing, securing health benefits for, and protecting all its legal citizens. Otherwise, the ruling body, whether elected or appointed, becomes a prejudicial theocracy and not an encompassing democracy.

Until recent years, I never doubted that the United States Constitution guarantees the free and lawful exercise of every American's religious or philosophical persuasions as long as they do not tangibly harm or debase others. Have I been wrong all these years? Are my desires and dreams for my beloved nation turning into a nightmare?

But let's not stop with America alone. Governments around the entire world should take immediate steps to safeguard the earth itself that is slowly dying amidst pollution, greed, and selfishness.

My Benefactor

Through the centuries, religion's long shadows have continuously darkened the pathway toward an optimistic future for this earth. And, at various times, these shadows have cast the form of a Jewish mezuzah or Star of David, a Catholic crucifix, a Protestant cross, an Islamic crescent moon and star, or other religious symbols of the world.

The swastika, for example, is a "symbol of the sun in the nature-religions of Aryan races from Scandinavia to Persia and India; and similar devices occur in monumental remains of the ancient Mexicans and Peruvians, and on objects exhumed from prehistoric burial mounds…[I]t is found invariably associated with the worship of the Aryan sun-gods (Apollo, Odin); it is believed to represent the sun. [It was] adopted as the German national symbol by the Nazis" (from *The Encyclopedia Americana*, 1961 edition).

As I walk humanity's shadowed way in my declining years, a dark cloud hangs overhead. It is the one that rains down hatred and mistrust on those of us who do not believe in either transcendent or immanent beings from outer space—that is, gods.

Because there are such gigantic problems in this world, I have a little difficulty in explaining the personal tranquility that comes from my nonreligious way of life. So many people and other animals are dying unnecessarily, being exploited, or simply existing in dreadful situations which I deplore. My heart aches for most of the world's inhabitants, yet I can honestly profess to you that the daily experience of unbelief provides for me a logical and appreciative lifestyle. I enjoy a contented, responsible, fulfilled life that does not involve a supernatural being. My activities and dealings with others are based on human morality and ethics, a foundation of mutual respect.

I admit, though, that at times it would be so much easier for me personally if I were still a Christian. Then I wouldn't be confronted with pity, disgust, or hostility from the larger believing world. I could, perhaps, pretend that I believe, but I would be living a lie. And my character recoils at even the thought of that.

So, yes, my experience of unbelief does make me happy. It is not a giddy, superficial happiness; it is a deep personal satisfaction that affords peace of mind. It makes me appreciate the time, however long or short, I have for the enjoyment of transient life. It inspires in me an appreciation for my own physicality and that of every living creature of the world in a way that religion never did.

I would be even happier if every man and every woman truly became my brother and sister, no matter how divergent our beliefs or non-beliefs are. For this to happen, it's going to take much more than any of us are doing now.

Finally, I want you to know that I cherish every moment of life. Yet I do not fear a nonexistent state into which I probably will one day pass at death. Until that moment is accomplished, I value even the smallest opportunities that come my way for eliminating bigotry or alleviating pain and suffering. I am grateful for any occasion presented for educating others regarding my experience of unbelief and its logic. I value every person who reciprocates my respect. I appreciate everything that benignly enhances my existence—for *life itself is my benefactor*. And what an experience that is!

Epilogue

Ode to a Freethinker's Wishes

I wish for freethinkers a kind, tranquil place
Where we could be free of all who disgrace
With tactics they hope will sully our name
And bring us all down in guilt and shame.
I wish for a place where in every season
We'd celebrate reality and encourage reason,
Where the golden rule would be purely untarnished
And absolute truth would be totally unvarnished.
I wish for a place where justice prevailed,
Where verity and fact are never assailed,
Where fairness for one is the same for all others,
And people would feel like sisters and brothers.
I wish there were schools where children could learn
To think for themselves, to perceive and discern
That religious fables and manmade creeds
Distort and deter what this world truly needs.

Epilogue

I wish for a place where, if taxes were taken,
There'd be genuine help for the poor and forsaken,
Where poverty and crimes might be things of the past
If every willing worker was paid fairly at last.
I wish for a place with air pure and clear,
Where we could drink water without dread and fear
Of poisons from factories and farms run by greed
And those who think little of a healthy earth's need.
I wish oil and coal companies would actively accede
To our planet's critical and crucial need
For natural, clean fuel in cars, trains, and homes,
In airplanes or ships and wherever one roams.
I wish the world's forests weren't being denuded
By those unaware or completely deluded
That their actions today have no application
To the future of all life in whatever nation.
I wish politicians would dispense with their airs
Of pretentious piety in government affairs.
I wish they would keep all religion at bay
For actions speak louder than whatever they say.
If there was a place like the one just described,
I'd really not need to be coerced or bribed.
I'd hightail it there just as soon as I could
And offer my help for every creature's good.
A communist? A socialist? Oh, no, not me—
Just an honest freethinker who longs to be free
Of religion's belligerence, its "holy" grails,
Its political flattery, and mythical tales.
I wish instead of hate, guilt and penitence,
We could share kindness in daily experience.
I wish for every creature and humans of each race
A beautiful, serene planet; an unbiased, safe place.

—© 2009 Betty Brogaard

Bibliography

Alper, Matthew. *The "God" Part of the Brain*. Brooklyn, NY: Rogue Press, 1996.

Barker, Dan. *Godless: How an Evangelical Preacher Became One of America's Leading Atheists*. Berkeley, CA: Ulysses Press, 2008.

———. *Losing Faith in Faith: From Preacher to Atheist*. Madison, WI: Freedom From Religion Foundation, 2006.

Basinger, David. *The Case for Freewill Theism*. Downers Grove, IL: InterVarsity Press, 1996.

Blaylock, Thomas E., Jr. *Honest Man's Philosophy: How to Analyze, Criticize and Modernize Philosophy with Honest Clear Thinking*. Bloomington, IN: AuthorHouse, 2005.

———. *The Night They Waked Uncle Bob: The Life of the Sheriff of Rex Parish*. Bloomington, IN: AuthorHouse, 2004.

Bouman, Herbert. *A Look at Today's Churches—A Comparative Guide*. St. Louis: Concordia Publishing House, 1980.

Boyd, Gregory A. *God of the Possible*. Grand Rapids, MI: Baker Books, 2000.

———. *Is God to Blame? Moving Beyond Pat Answers to the Problem of Evil*. Downers Grove, IL: InterVarsity Press, 2003.

Brogaard, Betty. *Dare to Think for Yourself: A Journey from Faith to Reason.* Baltimore: PublishAmerica, 2004.

Cherry, Matt, Tom Flynn, and Timothy Madigan, eds. *Imagine There's No Heaven: Voices of Secular Humanism.* Amherst, NY: The Council for Secular Humanism, 1997.

Comte-Sponville, Andre. *The Little Book of Atheist Spirituality.* New York: Viking, 2007.

Dawkins, Richard. *The God Delusion.* Boston: Houghton Mifflin, 2006.

———. *The Selfish Gene.* Oxford: Oxford University Press, 1976.

Dexter, Allen C. *Believing the Unbelievable.* Philadelphia: XLibris Corporation, 2006.

Doherty, Earl. *The Jesus Puzzle: Did Christianity Begin with a Mythical Christ?* Ottawa: Canadian Humanist Publications, 1999.

Freke, Timothy and Peter Gandy. *Jesus and the Lost Goddess.* New York: Three Rivers Press, 2001.

Graeser, Mark H., John A. Lynn, and John W. Schoenheit. *Don't Blame God.* Indianapolis, IN: Christian Educational Services, 1994.

Geisler, Norman. *Chosen but Free: A Balanced View of Divine Election.* Bloomington, MN: Bethany House Publishers, 2001.

Green, Ruth Hurmence. *The Born Again Skeptic's Guide to the Bible.* Madison, WI: Freedom From Religion Foundation, 1982.

Harris, Sam. *The End of Faith.* New York: W. W. Norton & Company, 2005.

———. *Letter to a Christian Nation.* New York: Random House, 2006.

Henderson, John A. *God.com: A Deity for the New Millennium.* Boone, NC: Parkway Publishers, 2005.

Humphreys, Kenneth. *Jesus Never Existed.* East Sussex, England: Iconoclast Press, 2005.

Joshi, J. T., ed. *Atheism: A Reader.* Amherst, NY: Prometheus Books, 2000.

Ludemann, Gerd. *Paul: The Founder of Christianity.* Amherst, NY: Prometheus Books, 2002.

Martin, Ernest L. *Progressive Revelation within the Bible.* Pasadena, CA: Foundation for Biblical Research, 1980.

———.*Restoring the Original Bible*. Portland, OR: Associates for Scriptural Knowledge, 1994.

Martin, Michael and Ricki Monnier, eds. *The Impossibility of God*. Amherst, NY: Prometheus Books, 2003.

Mills, David. *Atheist Universe: The Thinking Person's Answer to Christian Fundamentalism*. Berkeley, CA: Ulysses Press, 2006.

Novak, Michael. *No One Sees God (The Dark Night of Atheists and Believers)*. New York: Doubleday, 2008.

Perakh, Mark. *Unintelligent Design*. Amherst, NY: Prometheus Books, 2004.

Price, Robert M. *The Incredible Shrinking Son of Man*. Amherst, NY: Prometheus Books, 2003.

Russell, Bertrand. *The Conquest of Happiness*. New York: W. W. Norton & Company, 1996.

———. *Why I Am Not a Christian*. New York: Simon & Schuster, 1957.

Saranam, Sankara. *God Without Religion: Questioning Centuries of Accepted Truths*. Albuquerque, NM: The Pranayama Institute, 2005.

Smith, George H. *Atheism: The Case Against God*. Amherst, NY: Prometheus Books, 1989.

Wright, R. K. McGregor. *No Place for Sovereignty*. Downers Grove, IL: InterVarsity Press, 1996.

Zindler, Frank R. *The Jesus the Jews Never Knew*. Cranford, NJ: American Atheist Press, 2003.

Index

Index

F

Faith, 43, 53–54, 58–59, 123, 124, 125; in the Bible, 53–54, 98–99
Fatalism, 65
"Father," use of, 39–40
Fear, of God, 75
Feminism, 95–98. *See also* Women
First Amendment rights, 113–14
Forgiveness, 50–51
Formative doctrines, and the Bible, 90–92, 94
Free will, 116
Fundamentalist religions, 76, 79

G

Gandhi, Arun, 139–40
Global warming, 78
Glossalalia, 90–91
Goals, of atheists, 22–23
God, 62–71; as all-knowing, 115–19; and anger, 67–68, 74–75; and book of Job, 67–71; and evil, 65–67; existence of, 15, 33–35, 143, 146–147; fear of, 75; and good, 66; and Open Theists, 115–19; and Sabbath, 108; and Ten Commandments, 108–11; and violence, 62–65
God Without Religion (Saranam), 138–41
God's Problem: How the Bible Fails to Answer Our Most Important Question—Why We Suffer (Ehrman), 59–60
The God Delusion (Dawkins), 34, 127–28
Godless: How an Evangelical Preacher Because One of America's Leading Atheists (Barker), 143
Golden Rule, 61, 127
Good, and God, 66
Good works, in the Bible, 99–100
Gore, Al, 78
Grace, in the Bible, 99

Grace, saying at meals, 42
Graven-image commandment, 107–108

H

Happiness: and belief, 35–37; in the Bible, 56–57
Harris, Sam, 150
Haught, James, 77–78
Hawking, Stephen, 27–28
Heaven, 48–50, 54–55
Hell, 29, 46–48
Humility, and the Bible, 43–44
Humphreys, Kenneth, 137
Hussein, Saddam, 76–77

I

Immortal soul concept, 46–48
Immortality, 129
Intellectual growth, importance, 26–27, 73–74, 125, 126
It's a Wonderful Life (movie), 50

J

Jesus, 30, 48, 51, 53, 102, 105, 112, 119, 131; baptism, 117; crucifixion, 57, 102
Jesus Never Existed (Humphreys), 137
Job, 68–71, 116
John Paul II (pope), 144, 145–46
John the Revelator, 74–75
Judaism, and original Ten Commandments, 107, 108, 111, 113

K

King, Martin Luther, Jr., 157–58
Krauss, Lawrence M., 150–51

L

Latter-day Saints, and communion, 103
Learning, importance, 26–27, 73–74, 125, 126
Limbo, 145–46

Index

Other Books from Ulysses Press

Atheist Universe: The Thinking Person's Answer to Christian Fundamentalism
David Mills, $14.95
Foreword by Dorion Sagan
Clear, concise, and persuasive, *Atheist Universe* details exactly why God is unnecessary to explain the universe and life's diversity, organization, and beauty.

Godless: How an Evangelical Preacher Became One of America's Leading Atheists
Dan Barker, $14.95
Foreword by Richard Dawkins
In *Godless*, Barker describes the intellectual and psychological path he followed in moving from fundamentalism to freethought.

Deciphering The Lost Symbol: Freemasons, Myths and the Mysteries of Washington, D.C.
Christopher Hodapp, $12.95
Guides readers step by step through Brown's intricate novel while differentiating history and myth from pure fiction.

Do It Yourself Guide to Biodiesel: Your Alternative Fuel Solution for Saving Money, Reducing Oil Dependency, and Helping the Planet
Guy Purcella, $15.95
Contains the most current and complete information available for making biodiesel at home.

Mapping the Memory: Understanding Your Brain to Improve Your Memory
Rita Carter, $14.95
Helps readers reach a higher level of understanding about memory and how they can improve the working of their own brain function in this area.

Should I Eat the Yolk?: Separating Facts from Myths to Get You Lean, Fit, and Healthy

Jamie Hale, $14.95

There are literally hundreds of these little nuggets of advice floating around, and after hearing them over and over again, many people start to assume they must be true. But are they? In *Should I Eat the Yolk?* author Jamie Hale looks at over 200 of these claims and separates fact from fiction.

The Six Unsolved Ciphers: Inside the Mysterious Codes That Have Confounded the World's Greatest Cryptographers

Richard Belfield, $14.95

Brings to life the amazing stories and fascinating structures of the secret codes that have stubbornly resisted the efforts of the world's best code-breakers and most powerful decryption software.

Solomon's Builders: Freemasons, Founding Fathers and the Secrets of Washington, D.C.

Christopher Hodapp, $14.95

Solomon's Builders guides readers on a Freemason's tour of Washington, D.C., as it separates fact from myth and reveals the background of the sequel to *The Da Vinci Code*.

To order these books call 800-377-2542 or 510-601-8301, fax 510-601-8307, e-mail ulysses@ulyssespress.com, or write to Ulysses Press, P.O. Box 3440, Berkeley, CA 94703. All retail orders are shipped free of charge. California residents must include sales tax. Allow two to three weeks for delivery.

About the Author

Betty Brogaard is a former Evangelical church member and writer turned atheist. Her first book, *Dare to Think for Yourself*, was published in 2004. She lives in Wisconsin.